Troublemaker

A Memoir of Sexism, Retaliation, and the Fight They Didn't See Coming

Lisa Cornwell
with Tucker Booth

TRIUMPH
B O O K S

Library of Congress Cataloging-in-Publication Data available upon request.

This book is available in quantity at special discounts for your group or organization. For further information, contact:
    Triumph Books LLC
    814 North Franklin Street
    Chicago, Illinois 60610
    (312) 337-0747
    www.triumphbooks.com

Printed in U.S.A.
ISBN: 978-1-63727-256-5
Design by Nord Compo
Photos courtesy of Lisa Cornwell unless otherwise indicated

For my mom, who's always wanted me to write a book;

My dad, who's given me the courage to write this book;

Sarah, whose support made writing this book possible;

And for Melody and Chris, in loving memory of Sam.

Always aim high, work hard, and care deeply about what you believe in. And, when you stumble, keep faith. And, when you're knocked down, get right back up and never listen to anyone who says you can't or shouldn't go on.

—Hillary Rodham Clinton

CONTENTS

———

Foreword by Hillary Rodham Clinton   xi

Introduction   xv

Authors' Note   xix

Part I: Background

1 The Call. 3

2 The Younger Years
and a Kid Named Tiger. 17

3 POTUS. 23

4 The 3-Iron That Saved My Life. 33

5 The Unexpected Divorce. 41

6 Monster. 47

7 Facing the Demons. 51

Part II: Lights, Camera, Action

8   TV Life. 59

9   Dream Job. 65

10 The Boys' Club. 69

11 Relationships and Retaliation. 75

12 The B-Team. 81

Part III: Trouble in Paradise

13 Chamblee. 89

14 Sarah Kemp. 97

15 Outed. 103

16 Unscathed. 115

17 Husband and Wife. 119

18 The Final Straw. 125

19 The Beginning of the End. 129

Part IV: Shots Fired

20 Beware: HR. 137

21 The NBC Way. 147

22 Reality Hits Home. 153

23 The Untouchables. 159

24 Demoted. 171

25 Decisions. 175

Part V: Firing Back

26 Enter Tom Mars. 181

27 Dear David Cohen. 187

28 EEOC, Part I...................................191

29 Fruit Basket....................................197

30 EEOC, Part II..............................207

Part VI: Repercussions

31 January 2021.................................219

32 *Washington Post*..............................225

33 Solidarity.....................................239

34 The Aftermath..............................245

35 EEOC, Part III............................255

36 Case Closed...................................263

37 Lessons Learned.............................269

Afterword by Tucker Booth   275

Acknowledgments   289

About the Authors   295

FOREWORD

THOUGH GOLF IS a big part of Lisa Cornwell's story, this is not a golf book. You will appreciate it even if you've never played a round before.

I'm not an unbiased observer. I've known Lisa since she was a little girl in Arkansas, coming to our family Christmas parties at the Governor's mansion in Little Rock. Lisa is Bill's cousin by way of his grandmother Eula Mea Cornwell Clinton, whose family came to Arkansas from Mississippi on a wagon in 1898. There are lots of Cornwells in Arkansas now. Bill got to know them, including Lisa's parents, when they were young, and became friends. Most of the Cornwells were outgoing, high-spirited, and loved politics.

Even as a child, Lisa was a standout example. I'll never forget walking into our bedroom during one of the family parties to find little Lisa and her cousin in my closet trying on my coats. They were embarrassed, but I loved it, and never outed them to their parents. When Bill was elected President, I gave him a new set of Ping irons to go into the beautiful golf bag with the Presidential seal that Lisa had given him. He loved them, and for years afterward, Bill and Lisa tried to get me interested in golf without success. It's a hard game.

So is life. That's what this book is about.

When I was in law school, I developed a passion for empowering women, improving the lives of children, and strengthening families. I once chaired a committee for the American Bar Association, dedicated to achieving equal opportunity for women lawyers. And in 1995, when the U.N. Secretary General asked me to keynote the U.N.'s Fourth World Conference on Women in Beijing, the one sentence that captured the imagination of people and inspired them to action was, "If there is one message that echoes forth from the conference, let it be that human rights are women's rights and women's rights are human rights, once and for all."

In the years since, a lot of progress has been made, but as Lisa's book shows, there's still a long way to go. Thankfully, gutsy women are still at it the world over, and especially in the U.S. after the repeal of *Roe v. Wade*.

Lisa Cornwell is one of them. When she finished her college golf career, she decided that the endless travel of professional golf wasn't for her, and she went to work in sports broadcasting, eventually working her way up to Golf Channel. Bill loved watching her, because she knows so much about the game and the players. But she was also determined to use her platform to push for more equal treatment for women golfers. As you'll read, that's what finally turned her workplace from merely challenging, to toxic, driving her out of the job she loved and worked hard at, even to the very end.

Sadly, her experience is not uncommon and still too often unreported. Now, after years of causing what my late friend Congressman John Lewis called "good trouble" for others, Lisa, always a champion of the underdog, in the end had to stand up for herself—which is often a much harder task, especially when there's a media giant on the other side. That's what she's done with *Troublemaker*.

This is a thought-provoking, brave book, by a woman I liked as a little girl who grew up to be intelligent, honest, and strong. Reading it will make all of us more sensitive to discrimination still hiding in plain sight.

Hillary Rodham Clinton
February 2023

INTRODUCTION

We just think he's better than you.
> —Mark Summer, Sr. Director *Golf Central* (December 2018)

I **WROTE THOSE WORDS** on a piece of paper the day they were said to me and have had them taped to my computer at home ever since. How many women have heard comments like this from their bosses and felt unable to respond because of the person who said it? I'm usually not one to be at a loss for words, but I was that day. Even though I knew what Mark said wasn't true, it was still jarring to hear because the person who said it held all the cards...and had all the power.

On January 1, 2021, I *finally* put it out there. I'd wanted to speak publicly for a long time—about the injustices, the bullying, the nepotism, the discrimination, and the lies. There was so much I needed to say for all of us. The problem was, as a "public" television personality, I had to abide by their rules, mainly because of my contract. One wrong move, and I knew they'd come after me for violating our agreement.

Here's why: in 2019, after six successful years as an on-air personality for Golf Channel, owned by Comcast/NBCUniversal, I was being forced out. I'd been removed from assignments and was eventually demoted from a full-time employee to a freelance reporter, despite having nothing but positive reviews and a large following of golf fans who respected my work. Their reasoning? "Budget." Of course it was. It's the all-too-convenient excuse that companies give when they can't say otherwise.

The *real* reason I was being forced out? Because I spoke up. There were way too many issues of inequality and unfair treatment to remain silent. As a result, I became a thorn in the side of many on the management team, and slowly, I started noticing that my studio days were being reduced and certain assignments were being taken away. The following year, I was demoted.

But instead of crawling into a corner (which I sometimes wanted to do), I decided to challenge what was very clearly a case of retaliation—as you'll learn in great detail in the pages ahead. Later that year, in December 2019, I hired a lawyer named Tom Mars to represent me. Tom spent seven and a half years as Walmart's general counsel and two years running the company's HR department, so I had no doubt I was in good hands. In March 2020, we filed our first—of what would eventually become two—federal EEOC complaints citing several counts of discrimination and retaliation in the workplace while I still had a part-time, contractual job with the company.

It was career suicide. I knew it. Tom knew it. My family knew it. And at the time, writing a book about this experience wasn't even on my radar. But I was so far past the point of worrying about the aftermath and repercussions. What had happened to me—and dozens and dozens of other women at the network, I would soon learn—had to be exposed. Nine months later, I was terminated.

———————

For anyone thinking this is a golf book, it isn't. Yes, there are many references to golf because that was my job, and it's been a huge part of my life since I was a little girl. But the heart and soul of this book is addressing the real-life struggles women continue to face in the workplace—and that workplace can be in any industry, not just sports—and it must change. The only way I know to stop it is to talk about it as much and as openly as we can.

Now, more than two and a half years into this journey, I understand why women don't take on these battles against big corporations. They're expensive, they drag on forever, and they'll beat you down in a hurry. The character assassinations that Golf Channel/NBCUniversal has delivered in its EEOC responses alone would be enough to make anyone question herself and her abilities. I'll admit, I've allowed it to happen from time to time. But then I go back and re-read the messages I've received—from former co-workers to complete strangers—supporting this mission and reminding me that not only was I good at my job but, more importantly, I was fully dedicated to it even in the end when they continued to retaliate against me.

This book, and this battle, is for all the women who didn't have the support or the ability to take on Goliath. I promise to spend the rest of my life helping anyone who needs an ally in this arena as much as possible. It's also for the young girls who will unfortunately face this type of treatment in the workplace one day. I want them to know they're stronger than they realize and are supported by hundreds of thousands of women all around the world.

AUTHORS' NOTE

THROUGHOUT MY LIFE, I've stood up to bullies and those in authority who've had this uncanny ability to push people around and get away with it. When I was a freshman in college, I watched a large man hit a little woman as hard as he could in the face with a closed fist. Seconds later, I took matters into my own hands... with a 3-iron. I wasn't about to let him get away with what he did to that poor girl back then, just as I refuse to turn my back on any type of discrimination or unfair treatment today. As a result, I've been called a "troublemaker" more times than I can count. Why is it that women who stand up for themselves and others often get this label?

Recently, the public has been exposed to a series of sexual harassment cases involving high-profile, powerful men. In an era of unprecedented media sensationalism, the acrimonious downfalls of Harvey Weinstein, Bill Cosby, Matt Lauer, Les Moonves, Charlie Rose, and Andrew Cuomo have dominated the news cycles. While these shocking situations are worthy of close attention and fierce examination, it's important to recognize that most of the discriminatory acts committed against women have nothing to do with sex and are oftentimes just as abusive.

From homemakers to high-ranking executives, women are routinely taught that our input isn't welcome and when we do speak up, there are potential risks involved. This type of social repudiation forces a toxic choice upon us—either learn to keep quiet or kiss our chances of upward mobility goodbye.

During my seven years as an on-air host and reporter at Golf Channel, I made some powerful enemies by being a strong advocate for equality and fairness. Those enemies eventually conspired to push me and other women out because we refused to stay silent.

As of January 1, 2021, the first day I was no longer under contract with the network, my experiences have been well-documented. I've revealed some deep, dark secrets of a misogynistic culture—one where bullies and members of the boys' club got ahead while those of us who challenged the system got cast aside.

Soon after making my story public, upwards of 30 women contacted me privately about their own encounters and mistreatment. Unfortunately, most of these women have been unable to speak out because of nondisclosure agreements they signed after losing their jobs in order to receive a severance package. Others feared that voicing their struggles would blackball them in the industry moving forward. Trust me, I understand. Either way, it's both heartbreaking and infuriating.

My hope is that by revealing these truths in *Troublemaker* it unites women and brings about change; that the people running companies who repeatedly make unfair decisions toward women and minorities finally get exposed and are forced to change—or cast aside if unwilling to do so; that HR departments around the world become places that protect the employees, not their employers. It's astonishing how many people lack any sort of faith in their own HR departments to make their work lives better.

I want *Troublemaker* to serve as a reminder to these persecutors that we aren't going away. I want it to empower women who've been silenced out of fear of losing their jobs to speak up and to do it loudly. As Elie Wiesel so poignantly once said, "Silence encourages the tormentor, never the tormented."

May we all be (good) "troublemakers" together so that one day books like this will no longer be necessary.

PART I

BACKGROUND

————

CHAPTER 1

THE CALL

———————

I don't give a shit! I don't give a shit! You know what you need to do? If you're gonna be a reporter, you need to talk to both sides!
—Geoff Russell, Sr. VP Golf Channel (September 2020)

THE CALIFORNIA DESERT is indescribably different in September than early April, the latter being the time of year when I would typically be in Rancho Mirage. But 2020 was anything but a typical year. Besides being devilishly hot and not nearly as lush and green, it was also eerily quiet. All of this, as you might expect, was because of COVID.

Dating back to 1983, the ANA Inspiration held the honor of being golf's first major championship of the calendar year. This year, however, it was postponed because of the pandemic. Like most people around the world, I was deeply concerned about the virus. But I also needed to work.

When I was a kid, the ANA Inspiration was called the Nabisco Dinah Shore, and it had this magical allure to it in my eyes. The traditional winner's leap into Poppie's Pond is legendary, not just in the women's game but in all of golf. As a little girl who dreamed of playing professionally one day, it was bigger than The Masters to me. I can't tell you how many times I dreamed of joining all the players I looked up to by taking my own jump into the water surrounding the 18th green at Mission Hills Country Club. My championship formation would've been the cannonball because, unfortunately, I wasn't too creative in that department.

I'll never forget the first time I covered the ANA Inspiration for Golf Channel in 2015. Most of my enthusiasm came from how much I loved this tournament as a young girl. It was always my favorite event to watch and immediately became my favorite workweek of the year. This year, however, it emerged for two very different reasons. COVID was raging worldwide, and I was embroiled in the first of what would soon become two Federal EEOC (Equal Employment Opportunity Commission) charges against my employer. Life felt like a never-ending roller coaster.

At that point, my situation with Golf Channel had seemed to reach a precarious stalemate. I rarely communicated with the "powers that be" at the network, nor did they with me. In the meantime, I was doing everything I could to stay busy and keep my head up. If anything, in the most ironic way, the mandatory isolation due to the pandemic was a much-needed reprieve from battling them while also trying to work. I was able to stay home and attempt to get my wits about me, even though my recent struggles still occupied a large part of my thoughts. But as hard as I tried, I couldn't turn off all the internal turmoil. While many of my friends and family were understandably freaking out over their loss of livelihood, I was decompressing for the first time in years. As awful as that period was, the government shutdown and subsequent stay-at-home orders were actually a blessing in disguise for me personally.

When the 2020 ANA Inspiration rolled around, other than Golf Channel's desperate response to our original EEOC claim, it appeared as if the major players involved in the conflict had finally decided to try to play by the rules. To be clear, at no point did the glacial temperature between us even somewhat begin to thaw. They were merely honoring our contractual agreement, nothing more. Everything about my job was different now, though. I never heard from anyone in upper management. And other than an occasional text about the show from Mark Summer, the senior director of *Golf Central*, I was completely isolated from anyone in the "glass offices" at work. It was pretty clear that I was now on the tail end of my time at what used to be my dream job. But little did I know the next run-in with my superiors would be the most shocking of them all.

Five days before flying from Orlando to Southern California, I spent a few hours with an LPGA player named Xiyu (pronounced *she-yoo*) Lin. Xiyu is a Chinese player I'd gotten to know well over the years, although most of us call her "Janet"—an American nickname she'd given herself to make it easier for people to address her outside of her home country. In addition to being an outstanding talent on the course, Janet's also one of the nicest and most honest people I know. She'd never do anything to intentionally upset or offend anyone.

Sarah Kemp, another LPGA player who you'll be introduced to in greater detail later, was meeting Janet in Orlando that day to play a casual round of golf at a course called the Winter Park 9 and asked if I wanted to play, too. I usually said no to these invitations, but I decided to join them that day for some reason. When we met up, Janet quickly showed us the brand-new Mizuno irons in her bag. Now, if you aren't a golfer, it's worth noting that this was a significant change considering she was playing in a major championship in a little over a week. The day we got together was Janet's first time putting her new irons into play, and she couldn't have seemed more eager to do so… and also tell us the story about how they got there.

Before I get to Janet's story, it's worth noting that our casual nine-hole get-together wasn't too far removed from recent controversies involving racist and sexist rhetoric aimed at LPGA players. On his *PGA Tour Radio* show, Tiger Woods' former coach Hank Haney and his co-host Steve Johnson made disparaging, stereotypical remarks about Asian women:

> Steve: "This week is the 74th U.S. Women's Open, Hank."
> Hank: "Oh, it is? I'm gonna predict a Korean."
> Steve (laughing): "Okay, that's a pretty safe bet."
> Hank: "I couldn't name you six players on the LPGA Tour. Maybe I could. Well…I'd go with Lee. If I didn't have to name a first name, I'd get a bunch of them right."
> Steve: "We've got six Lees!"

This brazen display wasn't lost on my fellow journalists or me. In an op-ed for *USA Today*, Christine Brennan wrote, "If Haney is not fired from that job (and Johnson with him) and every other role he plays in golf and the news media by dinnertime…then the entire leadership of the game, the PGA Tour and Sirius XM is condoning racism, sexism and xenophobia while basically telling everyone who isn't a white male that golf is not the sport for them."

Hank Haney and Steve Johnson were fired by Sirius XM and *PGA Tour Radio* shortly after Brennan's scathing piece was published. Still, there had to have been continued psychological damage done to some LPGA players as a result, especially the Koreans and other Asian players. It wasn't as if these women hadn't already struggled with the knowledge that some in the golf world considered them less interesting, less exciting, and even less valuable than their white contemporaries. Haney's comments had merely spelled it out clearly for everyone to consider. To him, they were just nameless Koreans, not even noteworthy enough to take seriously during the week of a major.

While Janet never mentioned her feelings directly to me, I can safely assume that she repeatedly had to deal with many microaggressions here in the U.S. that only reinforced Haney's dismissive rhetoric. Much like America and the world at large, racism and sexism were once again exposed as significant problems in professional golf and society as a whole.

———————

I learned that day at Winter Park 9 that Janet had recently tested her new irons with a club fitter named Paris Fisher and her swing coach, Tony Zeigler. I didn't know Paris at the time, but I know Tony well. I've taken a lot of lessons from Tony over the years, and, like Janet, he's a great person. It'd be hard to find anyone who'd say a bad word about either of them. I'd trust these two people with anything I have, which is an important side note to this story.

After many hours of club testing a few days before we played together, Janet found a combination that worked much better for her than the irons she was using at the time. Tony and Paris agreed that she needed to make the change, even with a major championship less than two weeks away.

The next day, Janet, Tony, and Paris were all gathered in Paris' office in Orlando, and they made a call to the PGA Tour rep for Mizuno. They had to call him because, at the time, Mizuno didn't have a rep for the LPGA Tour. Janet asked Paris to start the conversation since she wasn't comfortable conveying exactly what she needed. I'd also assume that she felt intimidated by the social disconnect often accompanying those discussions. Janet was most certainly aware of the Hank Haney sympathizers who couldn't care less about the Asian players on Tour.

With Janet and Tony listening, Paris asked the rep if he could build the clubs she needed and get them to her quickly. According to them, all three of whom told me the story separately, the rep dismissively responded by telling them he didn't have the right components to get the irons built and sent out in time. Now, I can promise you this: if it'd been a PGA Tour player, getting the clubs wouldn't have been an issue. Still, Paris didn't give up easily. He asked the rep if Mizuno could just send him the iron heads, and he'd build them for her. The rep's response: "I'm sorry. I can't help you. I don't have what you need."

Three things are important to emphasize here. First, the tournament wasn't set to begin for 10 days, which was plenty of time to get the clubs to her. Second, Janet was in the top 30 on the LPGA money list and the top 100 in the world rankings, so she was playing very well—any manufacturer would've been crazy not to want her to play their clubs, especially in a major. Lastly, she wasn't looking for a sponsorship deal. She just wanted the clubs, which costs a company the size of Mizuno almost nothing. This sort of request is extremely common in professional golf.

After the rebuff, Paris tried one final option. He asked the rep if Mizuno could send Janet the heads, and she'd pay for them as well as the expedited shipping. Paris knew those heads were available to ship quickly somewhere in the company because they were commonplace items. The rep's final response: "Look, man…I'm not going to be able to help you, okay?"

By this point, Tony had heard enough of the conversation and angrily instructed Paris to hang up the phone. Seconds later, Tony called the manager he knew at a local golf store in Orlando and asked him if he had the clubs in stock, which he did. So, Janet headed there immediately and paid $800 for the set. Meanwhile, Paris called Nippon and asked if they could overnight the shafts to him. The answer: "Of course; no problem." The shafts arrived the next day, and he had her new irons built within hours.

Back on the first tee at Winter Park 9, right after Janet showed Sarah and me her new irons, she told us the story of what had happened with Mizuno and its impervious tour rep in detail. Sadly, it wasn't the least bit surprising. Not long before Janet's incident, Beth Ann Nichols wrote an article in *Golfweek* magazine detailing how Inbee Park, the No. 1 player in the world at the time, had asked TaylorMade for a few replacement woods and rescue clubs, and the company wouldn't give them to her. Instead, they offered to sell them to her at a discounted price.

"Park is a Srixon staff player but is only required to have nine Srixon clubs in her bag," Nichols wrote. "For more than five years she has played with four TaylorMade woods. That timespan includes six of her seven major championships, an Olympic gold medal, and more than 100 weeks as the No. 1 player in the world."

Do you think a male world No. 1 would have to pay for golf equipment? I think we all know the answer to that question. Most manufacturers and club fitters bend over backward to accommodate the men, delighting in the thought of building their brand awareness on television worldwide. When female players ask for the same considerations, they're often treated like nobodies.

"There has long been a great divide between the men's and women's game," Nichols continued, "It is also widely understood that sponsorship opportunities for LPGA players are vastly different. There's no pot of gold attached to a tour card. Blank hats and blank bags aren't limited to the lesser-known players."

"That's where we are," Park said at Royal Lytham. "It's frustrating, but there's nothing I can do at the moment."

Sadly, the type of dismissive behavior Janet encountered with Mizuno remains far too consistent with LPGA players. Still, the lengths to which Golf Channel and Mizuno would eventually go after I publicly revealed these concerning issues was nothing short of a character assassination attempt by both parties.

———————

Ten days after talking with Janet, I was in the on-air talent trailer in Rancho Mirage with my interview gear on—headset, microphone, and transmission pack—watching the morning wave of players in action during Round One of the ANA Inspiration and preparing for my first interview of the day. As I was getting ready to head to my one-on-one spot, just off the 18th green, I noticed Janet's name at the top of the leaderboard, and immediately my mind started racing. Anyone who follows me on Twitter knows that I'm not afraid to be outspoken, so I didn't think twice about sending out this tweet:

"The player leading the @ANAinspiration right now, Xiyu (Janet) Lin, put a new set of irons in the bag last week. @MizunoGolfNA wouldn't give them to her. She had to buy them. Incredibly disappointing."

Minutes later, I reached out to my producer, Beth Hutter, about wanting to interview Janet as soon as she finished. Unfortunately, she had a couple of bogeys coming in and dropped out of the lead, but I told Beth I still wanted to do it because I had some information about an equipment change that would be a worthy conversation. Beth, not knowing the story, gave me the green light to proceed. I could feel the adrenaline starting to kick in and, admittedly, was a little charged up about what I knew was ahead. Stories of unequal treatment like this need to be told, I kept reminding myself.

Janet let out an innocent giggle when she saw me there waiting to interview her after her round. A few minutes later, once we were both in place, Beth said in my earpiece: "Stand by, Lisa. You're next." I relayed the information to Janet, which I always did with anyone I was about to interview live, letting them know they were coming to us in a couple of seconds. As soon as the announcer sent the live coverage down to me, I led off with a statement before getting to the question—something like, "Janet…a very solid opening round with a new set of irons in the bag. I bet the Mizuno tour rep who made you pay for those clubs is regretting that decision right now."

Then, I shifted gears to her driving stats for the day and made that the focus of my first question since they were equally impressive. More importantly, I didn't want to put Janet in the uncomfortable position of having to address the point I'd just made regarding Mizuno. I got the jab in, which was my goal. She laughed a little and then tactfully answered the question about her driving that day without stirring the pot any further.

No, Janet didn't give Mizuno her credit card to buy those irons, which, as you'll later learn, is how Mizuno tried to spin the story by saying my words were factually incorrect. But because she wanted to use their irons that week, and the rep refused to give them to her, he essentially forced her to buy them. That was her only option. My comments, which I indeed meant as a stinging shot in the arm, came from my desire to highlight and then subsequently help eradicate this type of behavior. I didn't regret saying it then and wouldn't take it back now if I had it to do over again. It was tough talk but fair and accurate all the same.

I made those comments and sent out that tweet because what Mizuno had done to her was wrong, and the only way to get their attention was to call them out publicly. I was tired of waiting for other people to take up for women like Janet, especially minority women. Only recently, as this book is being written, has the issue of stopping

Asian hate even begun to permeate the public consciousness. Little did I know then just how much controversy was about to get stirred up because of my comments.

This was the first LPGA tournament I'd worked since my lawyer, Tom Mars, and I filed our original EEOC charge against Golf Channel. The entire situation made it hard to sleep that week. I knew I was being forced out by a small group of self-absorbed egomaniacs who didn't like that I spoke my mind, especially when it was about any type of inexcusable behavior. I relived all the slights and injustices that had happened at work the last several years over and over in my head. How could this still be happening, and why does it have to be this difficult, I kept asking myself. I was so tired of the battle yet never wavered from the mission.

Even though the tension with my Golf Channel superiors was thick, I was still excited for the 2020 ANA Inspiration. If anything, knowing my time with the network was ending, I was doing my best to appreciate every minute of the experience. It was a bittersweet week, and a big part of me already missed being there. But that "stopping to smell the roses" attitude went up in flames the day after my on-air interview with Janet.

I didn't get any negative feedback from Golf Channel about the tweet or interview the day they both happened, on Thursday. But I did get plenty of comments on Twitter thanking me for calling out Mizuno. I also received the same type of feedback from many of the players and caddies who know all too well how often this sort of thing occurs. At that point, I merely felt proud of standing up for Janet and all the women who've been slighted over the years. Since Mizuno didn't advertise with Golf Channel, I wasn't worried about any backlash there. I knew in my heart and in my head that I'd done the right thing. What I didn't know, however, was the massive storm that was now on the horizon as a result.

After the morning broadcast window ended the next day, I headed out to get some lunch. Shortly after dropping off my gear, I noticed I had a missed call from my direct boss, Geoff Russell, and my internal antenna immediately went up. I hadn't talked to Geoff in several months—long before filing my initial complaint with the EEOC—but I knew exactly why he was calling. Geoff's official title at Golf Channel was executive editor, yet he was listed as the person I directly reported to in the organizational chart for NBCUniversal. Oddly enough, he's also the husband of the woman who hired me, Molly Solomon, who remains the executive producer for the network.

A few minutes later, Geoff called again. I didn't answer because I've experienced that drive enough to know it would've been pointless. The cell service between the compound (where we worked) and the hotel was dicey at best, and I wouldn't have been able to hear him. Two minutes after the second unanswered call, he sent a text message asking me to call him. As soon as I was in the parking lot to pick up my to-go lunch, I sent him a text back saying that I was in a lousy area for cell phone service and would call him in 10 minutes from my room.

"OK," he responded.

By then, I 100 percent knew what was coming. I also knew that he wouldn't be able to control his temper. It was common knowledge around the office that Geoff would blow up when he got upset. I'd experienced it before and heard plenty of other stories affirming the same. I thought I was prepared for it, but I couldn't have been more wrong.

Now, back in my room, I made the call:

"Lisa. How are you?" he asked indifferently when he picked up.

"I'm fine, thanks. How are you?"

He paused. "Fine."

This conversation was already painfully annoying. Then he quickly got to the point.

"I'm calling about the tweet…forgive me, I'm spacing on the woman's name."

"Xiyu Lin," I replied.

There was a tense moment of silence.

"Janet," I tried again. "She goes by Janet."

"Yes," he finally confirmed. "Look, I'm calling because Mizuno was pretty upset about your tweet, and maybe they have a right to be upset. Did you reach out to Mizuno to get their side of the story as to why she had to pay for the clubs?"

"No," I responded calmly, "I talked to Janet, and she told me they just wouldn't give them to her."

"Who is Janet?" he asked again, obliviously.

I could feel my blood starting to boil. Geoff didn't give two shits about this scenario, or Mizuno, or Janet…he just wanted to nail me for something.

"Xiyu Lin…the player," I said in disbelief.

"Right. Did you talk to anyone from Mizuno about why she had to pay for the golf equipment?" he asked.

"No, I wasn't doing a story on it," I answered, "It's just a fact. It happens consistently on the LPGA Tour."

"But by putting out a tweet about it and saying it's disappointing, you're essentially doing a story about it," he said shortly. "Mizuno reached out to us and said you have misrepresented the story and are dragging them through the mud. There could be a lot of different reasons why she had to pay for the irons. Mizuno thinks…you are being unfair to them."

I was blown away but still somehow calm. I knew I had to stay that way because I could tell he was about to lose it. I could hear it in his voice.

"Geoff, let's think about this…. I'm being unfair to Mizuno when they made a top-ranked LPGA player pay $800 for irons? They're only upset because they have egg on their face. It happens all the time on the LPGA Tour. Beth Ann…Beth Ann Nichols wrote an article about it a couple of years ago when it happened to Inbee Park…"

That was it. That's all it took. The moment I knew was coming, when he absolutely exploded—interrupting me, shouting, *"Lisa! Lisa! Lisa!"*

"Geoff, hang on…I'm still talking." I remained calm, wanting to explain my side of the story. But he had no intention of hearing anything else from me and started screaming at this point.

"I don't give a shit! I don't give a shit! You know what you need to do? If you're gonna be a reporter, you need to talk to both sides!"

At this point, I interrupted him because he was not only way out of line but entirely out of control: "Okay, I'm hanging up. I don't have to stay on the phone and get berated by you again, okay?"

Geoff, still going at the top of his lungs, full of hatred and venom: *"You know what you're gonna do…you know what you're gonna do…?!"*

I knew I was close to reacting similarly to his out-of-control tirade, so I did what I said I would do. I hung up, in shock. Even though I thought I'd been prepared for his outburst, I really wasn't. As soon as I hung up, I called Tom. He couldn't believe it, especially considering our still-pending EEOC case. While I was talking with Tom, Geoff tried to call me back. Tom and I agreed not to answer, so I let it go to voicemail. A few minutes later, Mark Summer called, so I put Tom on hold and answered.

"Lisa, you have to call Geoff back," Mark demanded right away.

"Mark, I'm not going to get back on the phone with Geoff after that outburst," I said firmly. "You can tell him if he needs to communicate with me, he can do so through you or via text or email, and I'll respond. But that's it right now."

"Okay, I'll tell him," Mark grumbled, hanging up.

After I got back on the other line with Tom, who was still on hold, Geoff tried to call again. And again, I was undeterred and didn't answer. Tom agreed.

Five minutes later, Mark called me back. "Geoff wanted me to call you and tell you to come home."

I was almost speechless. "What? He's sending me home from the tournament?" I asked.

"Yes," Mark responded.

I've heard Mark talk to me enough over the years in a tone where he almost seemed proud to be delivering me bad news. This time was much different, though. He actually sounded embarrassed to be saying those words.

"So, let me make sure I'm getting this right. Geoff screamed at me...and cussed me out...and now he's sending *me* home?"

"Yes," he said quietly.

I calmly said, "All right," and hung up.

CHAPTER 2

THE YOUNGER YEARS AND A KID NAMED TIGER

My mother said to me, if you are a soldier, you will become a general. If you are a monk, you will become the Pope. Instead, I was a painter, and became Picasso.

—Pablo Picasso

GROWING UP IN ARKANSAS, I never considered myself inferior to the boys. This could probably be linked to a variety of factors. Like most kids I knew, my parents were great role models. My mom was a surgical nurse at the V.A. Hospital in our hometown before retiring after 45 years of service, and my dad was (and still is) an insurance agent. As you can imagine, he had a lot more flexibility with his day than she did. Because of that, our dad was the parent who made sure we were ready on time and ate breakfast before he took us to school. This created the impression to my sister and me early on that men and women were essentially equal. I honestly had no idea the depths to which sexism still existed until I got into the media in my early thirties.

But even more noticeable than my parents' example, I knew I could compete with boys. I spent my summers and after-school hours playing basketball, football, wiffleball, and kickball against the boys in my neighborhood and, to be honest, I was better than most of them. As I got older, I practiced and played with the boys at my local golf course, and in high school, I played on the boys' golf team because my school didn't have a girls' team at the time.

On the boys' side in the national junior circuit where I competed (the AJGA—American Junior Golf Association) there was a skinny kid named Tiger Woods. He was one year younger than me and quickly became a good friend. Unlike many of our peers, we both had middle-class upbringings and were big golf nerds.

There was something special about Tiger—even back then. I didn't realize it at the time and wouldn't have been able to explain it if anyone had asked. I just think as human beings, we're naturally drawn to successful people. But there's a significant difference between being successful and being a child prodigy. Picasso was a prodigy. So were Mozart, Bobby Fischer, and Shirley Temple. Little did I know that my friend would one day be listed among those once-in-a-lifetime talents.

While I was never as good as Tiger, I felt as though I wasn't too far behind him talent-wise, either. I laugh thinking about that now because I couldn't have been more wrong. Still, despite my achievements in other sports, including being a two-time All-State basketball player, it was pretty clear that golf would be where I excelled the most. Successful, yes. Child prodigy? Not even close.

Growing up around Tiger was probably not as mind-blowing as you might imagine. We were kids. We both loved Diet Dr. Pepper. Interestingly, I never asked him why he drank the diet version, although I did wonder, especially since he didn't have an ounce of fat on him. We both loved to listen to music while we practiced. But

I must admit that his musical appreciation was much more refined than mine at the time. He listened to jazz, and I was a top-40 junkie. I can still see that banana yellow Walkman cassette player in his ears and looped to the belt on his shorts like it was yesterday.

Tiger was different—not just because he was the only golfer among us with Black roots—but, when it came to golf, he treated the girls as though we were as good as the boys, including me. He respected our skills and appreciated the way we played the game. While he's a fierce competitor, he's also a mindful student of the game. Tiger was a nice kid, humble and respectful. He always called my dad "Mr. Cornwell." To this day, my dad still tells the story of when Tiger came up to him one afternoon during a practice round we were playing together in New Orleans and said, "Mr. Cornwell, I would give anything to have Lisa's swing." Now, I've never been under the impression for one second that Tiger actually meant what he said. I think he was just being nice. But my dad still believes it, and that's all that matters.

As much as I enjoyed the friendship Tiger and I had back then, I adored his dad just as much. Colonel Woods, as I always called him, became a mentor and teacher to me during those years. I don't know how to explain it, but Colonel Woods got it. He knew what it took to succeed, and I have no doubt that would've been the case in more instances than just golf.

After a late practice round one day at The Woodlands, a course just outside Houston, Texas, where we were both competing, Tiger and I were hitting balls on the driving range when suddenly, I felt something thump me lightly on the back. I turned around to see what had hit me and was perplexed to find Colonel Woods sitting on his pop-up chair, 15 feet or so away, staring at me intently. It was the kind of stare that I was too intimidated to question. So I turned back around and hit another shot. Thump. There it was again. I turned around once more, only to see the same stoic expression on Colonel Woods' face. *What's going on?* I thought to myself. I looked down by my feet, and there were two small pinecones, soberly laying there as if they were trying to tell me something. After thinking about it for a few seconds, I quietly whispered to Tiger, who was only five or six feet away, "I think your dad's throwing pinecones at me."

He took a quick look back at Colonel Woods, then glanced down at the pinecones before looking at me with this little wry grin on his face. "He must not like how you're practicing," he laughed, returning to his meticulous routine.

Knowing there was no other alternative, I gathered some courage and shyly walked over and stood next to the man I admired. "Colonel Woods, am I doing something wrong?" I asked, somewhat scared to hear the answer. He nodded slightly and then motioned for me to come closer. This was a former Green Beret in his element—teacher, instructor, psychologist.

"You have a great swing, Lisa," he began, "but the way you're practicing is limiting your improvement. Why are you in such a *damn* hurry?" Then he turned and pointed to Tiger, still engrossed in his work.

"Watch how he practices," he emphasized. "Look at how slow and methodical he is about it. Tiger takes his time, visualizing every shot he's going to hit. And then, he takes his time after each swing to think through what he did right or needs to do differently on the next one. On the other hand, you're hitting that bucket of balls like you're trying to get through them as fast as you can. You can't improve if you don't take the time to pay attention to each shot you hit, even in practice."

We both walked over to where I'd been hitting balls, and Colonel Woods showed me some techniques he was working on with Tiger. He was exactly right. My practice methods instantly improved after his lesson, and my game did, too. Most importantly, I knew from that moment on that Colonel Woods cared about me. He helped me a lot during those years. After the pinecone incident, I never hesitated to get his advice when something wasn't going right.

While I had no idea at the time that my junior golf friend would later become the best player in the history of the game, Colonel Woods never doubted it. He instilled that greatness in Tiger early on, metamorphosing from a child prodigy into the steely-eyed PGA Tour assassin he would become.

Unfortunately, life off the course hasn't always been as easy for Tiger. They often say with fame and fortune comes a hefty price. I can't imagine having my personal life scrutinized the way his has been over the years. Many books have been written and documentaries have been made about Tiger and his dad, more often than not painting a negative image of them both.

Tiger isn't perfect. None of us are. Yet we often treat these icons like they should be perfect without fail. Trust me, I'm not condoning the mistakes we make in life. But I do understand our flaws as human beings. As long as people try to learn from what they did wrong and become better than they were before, that's what matters most. And it's exactly what Tiger's done.

With Tiger and friends at the AJGA All-American Awards Banquet (1990).

I'm proud of my old friend and thankful we've been able to reconnect over the last several years. Every time we're together, it's like we're kids again—only now we joke about how old we're getting. When Tiger won his first Masters title in 1996, I teared up watching him give his dad a big bear hug after walking off the 18th green on Sunday. When he won his fifth green jacket in 2019, those same tears were back, but even bigger this time, watching him wrap his arms around his mom and children. Tiger had overcome all sorts of odds when many in the sports world had written him off. But most importantly, the smile he showed was as genuine as it's ever been. He was happy, and the world got to see a glimpse of the person I've been fortunate to know all these years.

CHAPTER 3

POTUS

MOST PEOPLE WOULD probably assume that becoming one of the country's best junior golfers and being a childhood friend of Tiger Woods were the most noteworthy events of my early years. But surprisingly, they paled in comparison to what would happen next.

While I was making a name for myself on the golf course, a relative of mine was making a worldwide name for himself in the political arena. Little did I know then just how far-reaching the name Bill Clinton would become. As a kid, it was pretty cool to brag that my dad's cousin was the Governor of Arkansas. And because he was my dad's cousin, that made him my cousin, too. Even better, I thought!

Every year, as far back as I can remember, we'd go to the Governor's Mansion in Little Rock for a big family Christmas party, and, occasionally, we'd see Bill at different events or fundraisers—mainly fish fries. Bill loves golf as much as I do, and he'd always send my dad notes and cards recognizing my achievements. I was very young at the time, and, because we lived so far away from Little Rock,

With my Aunt Dot; Bill; and Bill's mom, Virginia
Kelley, at the Arkansas Governor's Mansion
(Little Rock, Arkansas, December 1983).

I didn't really know him other than the family parties, campaign
stops, or whatever I saw or read in the news. But that all changed
on November 2, 1992.

I was a freshman in college at Southern Methodist University
in Dallas, Texas, and it just so happened that my cousin, who'd
become the Democratic nominee for President of the United States,
was making his final campaign stop nearby in Fort Worth before
flying back to Little Rock for Election Day. He'd been campaigning
hard on this final push. Defeating an extremely popular incumbent
seemed almost impossible, especially after taking blow after blow
in the media. But, like him or not, Bill Clinton's a fighter, and his
ability to personally connect with the voters may be better than any
candidate in American political history. A town hall debate with
President George Bush and Ross Perot just a few weeks before the

election would change Bill's life forever. And, in a sense, it changed mine, too.

I told my dad I wanted to go to that midnight rally on November 2 and asked if he could call someone in the campaign to get me up front so I could see Bill after it ended. Following an enthusiastic speech that lasted over an hour, he did his usual "Bill Clinton thing" and shook hands, took photos, and told stories with as many people in the first few rows of the packed audience as he could. That took almost another hour. I waited patiently and watched him intently, knowing I'd possibly be the last person he'd greet before walking 200 feet or so to his plane that would take him home.

When he saw me, he lit up. He put his hands on my shoulders, and his eyes started to get a little teary. He hugged me and then enthusiastically asked if I could get to Little Rock for Election Day. He leaned in and whispered, "We've just seen the latest polls. I think we're going to win tomorrow, and I want you to be there."

I was so stunned when he told me that it took a few seconds to fully process. *My cousin…was going to be…the next President of the United States.* I got on a flight the next day and the rest, as they say, is history.

I have no doubt being at the rally in Fort Worth that night played a significant role in the deep bond we have today. Bill and I are very close. Even though I don't get to see him as much as I would like, we talk and text quite often. He's been a great friend, confidant, encourager, adviser, big brother, and father figure all rolled into one. He's also been one of my favorite golf partners over the years.

On Christmas Day 1992, just a few weeks before Bill was sworn in, I drove down from my parents' house in Fayetteville to Little Rock to play golf with Bill in the snow and sleet with Hillary's two brothers, Tony and Hugh. This is another day that would change my life forever, mainly because of Hillary.

(Left to right): Tony Rodham, Bill, me, and Hugh Rodham
(Christmas Day 1992, Chenal Country Club, Little Rock,
Arkansas)

I was still freezing from the 18 holes we played earlier that day.
None of us could believe Bill wanted to finish the round. He loved it!
After it was over, we all loaded up in the motorcade and headed back
to the Governor's Mansion—which, even on Christmas Day, was buzz-
ing because of the transition. Bill went somewhere to make calls that
afternoon, and I went into the kitchen to try to find something hot to
drink and get a snack. When I walked in, Hillary was there and asked
me how the day went. I told her Bill was crazy to want to play golf in
that weather, and she nodded in agreement. Then she helped me make
some hot tea. While the water was boiling, she grabbed a jar of peanut
butter and asked if I wanted some. "Yes, please," I said. I was starving.

The next thing I knew, we each had a spoon and were taking
turns scooping out bites and making small talk. Even though I didn't

know Hillary nearly as well as Bill, I knew she was comfortable with me. She also knew how much Bill and I connected because of golf. Before our peanut-butter-eating marathon ended, she looked directly at me and said these words, which I'll never forget: "Lisa, Bill's life is about to change in ways I'm not sure he realizes just yet. He loves you and enjoys playing golf with you so much. I want you to promise me that you'll come to the White House to visit. You're always welcome. And if you ever need help paying for a ticket, let me know. We'll take care of it." I'll forever be grateful to Hillary for saying that to me back then. I honestly don't know if I would've felt comfortable enough to schedule trips to the White House on my own otherwise.

As you can imagine, the next eight years were filled with unforgettable experiences—from the dozens of nights I spent at the White House to riding in a presidential motorcade to being on Air Force One. During those years I also watched Bill navigate through some rough waters, both personally and politically.

It was all pretty intimidating at first, to be honest. The number of people who follow the president—personal assistants, security detail, the press corps, etc.—is enormous. Of all the experiences, though, nothing was more eye-opening than riding with the president in what's known as "The Beast." The presidential limousine is basically a dressed-up tank with thick bulletproof glass windows and body armor that could take on an array of fierce intrusions. It's comfortable inside, but I always found it impossible to sit back and relax. When the president is moving, everything else stops. All the roads are cleared for the motorcade to pass, which could include up to 50 other vehicles. Seeing cars halted at red lights with police officers and barricades set up to prevent anyone from getting anywhere close to the motorcade is an incredible sight and a reminder of all that goes into protecting the most powerful person on the planet.

As time went on during Bill's presidency, I became more at ease with him being the leader of the free world. Even though playing golf with snipers in trees isn't ever normal, it eventually became expected, and it was oddly comforting knowing that he was safe. Being on the top balcony of the White House, just off the solarium, having coffee only to look up to see armed guards staring into binoculars was part of it.

While collectively all of these experiences over his time in office were extraordinary, the most eventful time for me personally involved an incident that had me in hot water with the United States Secret Service.

It took place just over a year after the Monica Lewinsky scandal. Understandably, I hadn't heard much from Bill during the media turmoil and impeachment trial. I was worried about him but knew he had a lot to deal with publicly and privately. When the dust finally settled, I reached out to Bill and Hillary's most trusted personal assistant about coming up to stay for a weekend. After we decided on the date, I asked her if it'd be okay if a few of my close friends could meet me at the White House on that Saturday so I could give them a tour. She was fine with the request, thinking the company might do him some good.

I flew up with my friends to D.C. on a Friday and stayed with them that evening in a hotel. The next morning, I packed up all my stuff because I was spending the next two nights at the White House. We made the short walk over together since they were coming in for the tour and a quick meet-and-greet with the president—or so we thought.

We arrived at the Northwest Gate, went through all the usual background checks and clearance procedures, and then were ushered to the West Wing. Bill had just finished giving his Saturday morning radio address and was making some calls while we waited outside the Oval Office and chatted with his personal secretary, Betty Curry. Betty always treated me like family, and it was great to see her again after such a long time away between visits. Before all hell broke loose, I would visit every four or five months, depending on Bill's schedule.

Not long after we arrived, Bill, casually dressed, opened the door from Betty's office to the Oval Office and greeted everyone warmly. I could tell his guard was down, and he was happy to see us. He needed some friends from home at that moment, even though my friends were strangers to him. I couldn't believe how much he wanted to talk that day. He told stories at Betty's desk for 15 or 20 minutes before inviting us all into the Oval Office, where he told even more stories. To my surprise, many of them had to do with what he'd just been through. His candor was incredible, and I was relieved to know he was in a good place. Bill was having such a good time that he called and asked one of the butlers from the residence to bring his Chocolate Lab "Buddy" down so we could see him. We all went outside his office, where he continued to tell stories as we took turns throwing a tennis ball to his beloved pup.

After spending more than an hour with the president in the West Wing and thinking he was saying his goodbyes to my friends before he and I headed out to play golf, he surprised all of us with a curveball invitation. "Would you like to come back tonight and watch *Fight Club* with us?" he asked. My friends, of course, were thrilled, to say the least, immediately agreeing to come back. They couldn't believe it. Little did I know that watching *Fight Club* with my friends and the President of the United States wouldn't be the only unexpected event of the evening.

That night, Bill was in his element. Even though he was now in his second term, his Arkansas hospitality hadn't waned one bit. I went downstairs to greet my friends when they arrived, and Bill told me to bring them up to the residence and show them around. By the time we reached the solarium on the top floor, Bill was already there watching an Arkansas football game. When it ended, we all made our way to the movie theater in the East Wing of the White House.

POTUS or not, Bill wanted to make sure my friends and I were having a good time. He buzzed around the theater, offering us all popcorn, apple pie, and blankets. He was genuinely excited to see how much fun we were having. The massive screen and big plush theater seats to go with the booming sound system made the experience even more magnificent.

When the movie ended, we all thanked him and gave hugs, and he said his goodbyes. He told me to walk my friends out and that he'd meet me in the solarium later. He had a call to make. I would later find out that call was to Boris Yeltsin. Anyway, after escorting my friends out the Northwest Gate and saying our goodbyes, I started making my way back toward the residence. Then I heard my friend, Laurie Jo, call my name.

"Lisa! Lisa! I think I forgot something inside," she said.

I could see all my friends now standing outside the North Gate, but I was far enough away that I couldn't quite make out everything Laurie Jo was saying. So instead of walking on the sidewalk and around, I cut across the lawn to talk to her. That's when it happened. The second I took my first step onto the grass, the sky lit up with floodlights and alarm bells began blaring. Suddenly, camouflaged snipers emerged from the trees, and I could hear someone shouting on what sounded like a megaphone: GET DOWN ON THE GROUND, MA'AM...GET DOWN ON THE GROUND...NOW!

Out of nowhere, uniformed Secret Service agents came running from every angle. Unbeknownst to me, I'd set off the security sensors beneath the grass on the North Lawn and triggered a full-blown emergency intruder response.

Scared out of my mind and down on all fours, I pressed my face into the ground and waited for the agents to tell me what to do next. Meanwhile, a crowd was gathering outside the massive fence, trying to figure out who'd just illegally entered the White House grounds. Thankfully, I was wearing my all-access overnight guest badge, so the Secret Service didn't go into full arrest mode when they picked me up. Instead, they escorted me to the guard shack at the Northwest

Gate and followed the proper protocols and procedures to get me back inside.

After an insanely nerve-jangling 30 minutes to get cleared, I was released and escorted back to the residence. Worried that Bill was going to be upset about my literal misstep, I was relieved when I saw him waiting for me with a grin on his face.

"Sounds like you had a little trouble on the North Lawn," he joked. Once the shock wore off, we had a good laugh about the whole ordeal.

I understand there will always be people who criticize my cousin. Trust me, I've grown used to it over the years. And in this day and age, it's gotten even worse with social media. People refuse to have open and thoughtful conversations about politics anymore, which I believe makes us more defensive and less educated than in years past because we aren't listening to the other side. As Bill's late mother-in-law, Dorothy Rodham, once told him after he pressed her on why she regularly watched Fox News during his presidency, "Because you aren't always right, Bill." Just think how much better politics and this country would be if that logic still existed today.

I have no doubt many readers of this book will attack me because they hate my cousin...or Hillary...or both. They'll focus on the issues they believe justify them in their repugnant language—criticizing Bill or Hillary as political figures and, even worse, as human beings. I'm not going to get into all of it in this book, but I will say the millions upon millions of dollars spent over the years trying to take down the two of them is mind-blowing...and it's produced nothing. Any level-headed person has to realize that if something had been there—from Whitewater to Emailgate—they would've found it. But they never did.

Most importantly, as it pertains to this book and to equality in the workplace, my cousin was a changemaker. During the majority of

Bill's time as governor, he had a female chief of staff by his side, which was unheard of back then. During his eight years as president, nearly half of his administration's nominees were women. Most notably, he appointed the first female secretary of state in U.S. history, the first female attorney general, and the first female press secretary. He made equity and equality a priority. Thirty years later, much of America seems to have a difficult time following suit.

On a personal level, Bill has helped guide me through some of my darkest days, which you'll soon learn about. There was one issue in particular that I remember confiding in him about one night at the White House. After hearing what I had to say, I knew he was concerned about me. He wanted to do anything he could to help, including offering to call my parents to talk to them about it and show his support, which meant the world to me then and still does. To this day, I often call him to get his advice on the most important issues in my life.

I've learned a lot by watching Bill over the years—how he's handled criticism, controversy, defeat, and personal loss. When all of this came out about Golf Channel, he told me he was proud of me for standing up for myself. But he also strongly encouraged me not to let my anger get the best of me. He told me the story of Nelson Mandela, who spent 27 years in an apartheid prison. When he was released all those years later, Bill asked President Mandela if he felt hatred toward his captors. Mr. Mandela told him he did at first but then he realized as he was walking away from jail and toward freedom that if he carried that hatred with him, he'd still be their prisoner. He said he wanted to be free, so he let the anger go and advised Bill to always do the same. Bill passed that advice on to me not too long ago, and I've thought about it every day since. Being free from anger is a beautiful gift, but one that we can only give to ourselves.

CHAPTER 4

THE 3-IRON THAT SAVED MY LIFE

IT WAS A COOL fall evening in Fayetteville. I loved being home. It was my safe place. I remember looking up at what appeared to be thousands of stars in the sky that night, something that happened quite often in the small town where I grew up. For some reason, I recall how those stars were shining even brighter that evening. In a strange way, it felt like they were trying to speak to me. When I was a little girl, I talked to the stars constantly, but this was the first time I'd ever sensed they were actually talking back. I think something out there was trying to tell me that everything was going to be okay.

Like most weekends, I was home because I hated college. Only a few months had passed, and I'd already dipped into bouts of isolation and was discouraged in my new universe. I'd quickly gone from one of my town's most transcendent stars to a wayward satellite, rocketing toward what seemed like an endless black hole of despair.

Looking back, it should've been a time of excitement and celebration. I had a full golf scholarship to Southern Methodist University in Dallas—one of the most prominent academic schools in the country. A single semester's tuition at SMU was more than the new white Acura Vigor my parents bought me, which I knew they couldn't afford. But they always sacrificed for my sister and me. In hindsight, I think it was more of a thank-you gift for getting my college paid for. Of course, that was thanks to them as well. Like most teenagers, I was completely clueless about how real life worked.

After becoming the youngest person to ever win an Arkansas State Golf Championship at the age of 14—a record that still stands today—I spent the rest of my high school years dominating golf in my home state, winning three more titles before graduating. There were countless newspaper articles, TV interviews, and receptions honoring my achievements. Oddly enough, I'd already grown tired of the attention. I just wanted to hibernate from everything, even though I knew that was impossible. Because of my early success on the course, everyone expected me to go on to play college golf and then find stardom on the LPGA Tour. They thought it was "meant to be," whatever that means. While it broke my heart to leave home because the University of Arkansas didn't have a women's golf program, I left Fayetteville after signing with SMU, which was only a six-hour drive away.

I struggled to fit in from the very beginning. I grew up in a middle-class family, and SMU is anything but middle-class. It's a campus of brand-new BMWs and top-of-the-line handbags. So yes, I was a little intimidated by my surroundings. Beyond those struggles, I was also worried about my parents. They worked incredibly hard but couldn't seem to catch a break.

As mentioned earlier, my mom was a longtime surgical nurse at the V.A. hospital. She was wholeheartedly committed to her job, just as she was, and still is, to her family. For that reason, and so many more, she's a shining example of the positive impacts that working women have in this world. My mom went to work at seven o'clock every morning, Monday through Friday, and spent most weekends on call. I wish I had a dollar for every time I heard our phone ring in the middle of the night summoning her into work or every time I woke up not knowing that she'd been called in for emergency surgery. But she never complained about it. Ever. Because of her early alarm clock during the week, my dad took my sister and me to school every day— which I liked since that often included stopping to get donuts because he was the dad, not the mom, worrying about what we were eating.

Also, as previously mentioned, my dad's in the life insurance business. To this day, he's still the best man I know. He loves people and loves to talk. I've never known anyone who could take interest in another person or group of people as quickly as he does. He definitely has the gift of gab. There's no doubt I'm my mother's daughter in that area. I'm a listener, which makes it very perplexing why I chose to pursue an on-air television career. I guess that makes me a real-life oxymoron.

In addition to being a talker, my dad's also a very trusting person with a big heart. He makes friends easily, which unfortunately led to some regrettable financial decisions. When I was just six or seven, he decided to venture into the restaurant business. He was close friends with a man in our hometown who owned a local hotspot called King Pizza and thought its popularity could spread around the state. He was right. In just a matter of years, my parents had opened five franchises, and they were thriving. My sister and I liked it because we could eat all the pizza we wanted, and the salad bars were made from the scraps of old Model-T trucks.

Because the business was booming and my dad wanted to expand quickly, they brought a business partner on board, which would end up changing the trajectory of everything. My dad, being the person he is, put a lot of faith in this man, and, sadly, he caused the business to nosedive in no time. It was gross mismanagement from the moment he came on board—their best employees quit, food sales dropped dramatically, and their expenses started climbing out of control. The entire business almost collapsed. They became so desperate that my mom had to quit her job as a nurse to run the day-to-day operations because there wasn't enough money to pay anyone they trusted to come in and do it full-time.

My parents almost lost everything. It was more than two people could handle. I remember bill collectors coming to our house and ringing the doorbell. One winter, the heater in our house stopped working, so my parents bought space heaters for every room until my dad finally gave in and asked my grandparents for a loan. I could tell he was demoralized to have to make the request. But he never gave up. He also refused to file bankruptcy—stubbornly, as my mom would say. He believed in paying his debts, no matter what. And he did, every last penny. I still don't know how their marriage survived, especially now as an adult, and understanding the strangling pressure that not having enough money to pay your bills can put on a person. Thankfully, they're happier now than I ever remember them being before. They'll always be two of the strongest, hardest-working people I know.

So back to that starry-skied night in my hometown. I wasn't looking for trouble. I swear to God, I don't have a mean bone in my body unless I'm provoked. But wherever I go and whatever I do, trouble seems to have this interesting way of finding me. I think it's God's way of challenging me to step up. Life keeps nudging me to speak out when I see immoral behavior. That evening, I witnessed the most immoral act I've still *ever* seen in person.

The boys' and girls' basketball teams each had games, so I decided to go and catch up with some of my old teammates and coaches. I desperately missed being a part of a team and all those hours spent in practice together working hard for one goal.

The air in the gymnasium was especially ripe, permeated with the aroma of fresh popcorn and pungent sweat. As the players raced up and down the court, their high tops squeaked in concert with the crowd—a sound that was better than Beethoven to my ears. It was basketball, and I felt more at home than I had for a long time. When it was over, this sense of deep sadness took over. I remember the urge of wanting to get out of there quickly. I didn't want to stick around and talk to anyone. I just wanted to go home and be alone with my thoughts.

After the girls' game ended, I went outside to the parking lot to leave. As I got close to my car, which wasn't far from the side door where I exited, I saw a crowd of students gathered nearby. Before I could fully wrap my mind around what my eyes were seeing, a guy—who must've been at least 6'3"—pulled his long, right arm back and punched a girl—who was at least a foot shorter than him—square in the face with a closed fist.

The crowd watched uncomfortably, but no one stepped in to stop this madman. I felt an immediate surge of rage run through my body. To this day, I've never experienced anything quite like it. I could feel this fearless indignation take over my body. He was *hurting her!*

I rushed to my car, opened the trunk, and went straight for my 3-iron. I never went anywhere without my golf clubs back then. After all the hours I'd spent using them, I knew this guy—even as big as he was—didn't stand a chance. I had a battle ax in my grasp that I knew like the back of my hand, and it was all I needed. Carrying it like a sword, I stormed over to the altercation without hesitation. Everything at that moment suddenly went silent. All the sadness I felt just seconds prior had been overtaken by extreme focus. I was in my element. *"Hey, asshole!"* I yelled. *"Leave her alone!"*

This monster turned and glared at me. I could almost read what he was thinking: *How dare this little bitch come at me?* His focus immediately shifted from his victim, who was noticeably in a lot of pain lying on the hood of a car, and took a powerful step toward me. I could see his massive hand coming straight for my throat. This perpetrator, who was at least a foot taller and 50 pounds heavier than me, was determined to make me his second victim of the night.

With one hand around my throat, he bent down and appeared to be going after something with his other hand. My mind immediately jumped to the assumption he was reaching for a rock or some other blunt object. Still, no one in the crowd jumped in to stop him.

For all I knew, he was going to kill me. As he stood up, my instincts took over. I struck him as hard as possible in the shin with the hosel of my 3-iron. There was a sickening crunch of steel on bone. He immediately released me from his grip, grabbed his leg, and started screaming in pain. Clutching his gashed leg, he limped off, utterly demoralized. The girl he punched in the face ran into the bathroom inside the gym as fast as she could. Once I knew he was gone, I ran after her to make sure she was okay.

To this day, two things still stand out to me about that story. First, my initial emotion when I saw the assault wasn't fear. *I was livid.* As I've said before, I detest bullies, especially more powerful men who pick on and abuse women or kids. Every cell in my body wanted to stop what he was doing to her. There were no competing emotions. There was no desire to gawk at the injustice or tell myself that it wasn't my place to stop it. No "let the authorities handle it" logic to argue my way out of putting myself in the middle of danger. My parents raised my sister and me to fight when we saw injustice, so I guess you could say it's in our blood.

The second thing that still blows my mind is that no one—not a single guy or girl in the crowd of onlookers—tried to stop the attacker. Nobody even yelled for him to stop or for someone else to help. They all just stood there and watched, like it was some sort of shock and awe form of entertainment. That poor girl could've been killed. I guess, in reality, I could've been, too.

Just minutes after the incident, one of the assistant principals made his way to the scene and asked me to come to his office to talk about what had just happened. He started by asking if I was all right. I said I was still rattled but thankfully had no serious injuries. Then he told me the school knew who the guy was who'd attacked her and that the police had been contacted. Before I left, he thanked me for defending the girl and gave me a big bear hug. He was a great man and always looked out for his students, past, and present. I still miss him to this day. I wish I'd known that would be the last time I'd ever see Coach Hampton. He died unexpectedly a few months after that encounter.

Whenever I tell this story, people often marvel at me thinking I had any shot at stopping the violence that night. They ask skeptical questions about why I hadn't been more concerned about my own well-being. They say I was crazy but brave for bringing a golf club to a street fight. And you know what? They're probably right. If standing up to vicious attackers is crazy, I may be one of the craziest women out there. One thing's for sure, though. I'll never stop sticking my neck out when confronted with injustices like what happened that night in the parking lot. Everyone in that circle of spectators should've been just as upset as I was watching it happen.

To this day, I'm easily rattled by abuse. Seeing a bigger man hit a much smaller woman with a closed fist just 50 feet from me is an image that will forever be ingrained in my mind. I can still hear the sound of it, too. I realized that night that I'd never just be a spectator of wrongdoing and would always fight to protect myself and others at all costs.

CHAPTER 5

THE UNEXPECTED DIVORCE

I **DEFINITELY WASN'T YOUR** ordinary kid. Looking back, it's easy to work out that most of my belief system was built on the early success I had in sports. I craved those pats on the back from adults, whether I knew them or not. I believe that's what the experts would call a flawed sense of purpose. As long as I can remember, I've been a people pleaser. When things weren't going well at home, I figured my success on the golf course could erase those worries. I thought one more trophy or article in the newspaper, or someone coming up to my mom or dad telling them how proud he or she was of me, would be all they needed. Those things made me feel good because they seemed to make them feel good, too. But it's certainly not a healthy way for a kid to function. My parents didn't do it to me. I did it to myself, unknowingly.

Like many young girls, I started having body issues as a teenager, which led to long stares into full-length mirrors throughout the day. I didn't tell anyone about my newfound obsession. What did I look like in these jeans versus the other jeans? Were my thighs getting too big? What about my waist size? It was never-ending.

When I was a senior in high school, food issues also started coming into play. I told myself and my family that I was just "being healthy." Everything I put into my mouth was fat-free, sugar-free, and basically taste-free. Picante sauce poured onto plain rice cakes with a can of tuna was a typical lunch. Dinner usually consisted of steamed chicken, steamed vegetables, and steamed rice with low sodium soy sauce for flavor. That's how I rewarded myself. Fat-free/sugar-free ice cream was an occasional splurge. On Sunday nights only, I allowed it. My parents were growing tired of and angry at my food choices, but I wouldn't budge. My sister thought I was over the top. She was tall and thin and ate cheese dip and guacamole every day. I despised her for that.

It wasn't just my new way of eating that had them concerned. I'd also started working out like I was training for a triathlon—only my body wasn't being fueled for this type of endurance test. Every day of the school week, after a two-hour basketball practice, I'd go to the gym and put myself through a rigorous weight-lifting regimen, followed by running three miles on the treadmill. Around Christmas that year, my body fat had dropped so significantly that I stopped having my period. Like many things, I kept that from my parents, too.

Because of my food and fitness compulsion, my focus in life had changed entirely at this point. I cared more about working out and going for long runs than playing golf. The upcoming summer was supposed to be my real breakout year. Everyone expected me to dominate, especially considering I'd started taking lessons from world-renowned golf instructor David Leadbetter in Orlando the year prior. David was at the pinnacle of his career with many of the best players in the professional ranks as his pupils, and I'd recently become just the second junior player he'd agreed to work with—and it came with a hefty price tag. After almost a year of flying back and forth to see David, rapidly rising to No. 2 in the U.S. junior girls' rankings, and being named an AJGA First Team All-American for the second straight year, I didn't have the courage to tell my parents that I didn't want to do it anymore. I cared more about running bleachers in the hot sun and doing push-ups until I collapsed than I did about playing a game everyone expected would soon become my career. But I chose to keep going because I didn't want to let anyone down, continuing to compete while practicing less and less, and my results were start-ing to show it.

I remember vividly being at a tournament in California with my mom. It was one of the rare times that she traveled with me and not my dad, so it should've been a special week for the two of us to be together. Sadly, there weren't too many moments in my life at that point that came anywhere close to conjuring up those types of positive emotions. Even though we didn't talk about it, I knew they occasionally had to borrow money from the bank to pay for my golf tournaments, lessons, and all sorts of golf-related expenses. I tried to pretend I wasn't a burden. But deep down, I knew I was, especially now, considering that I didn't want to do it anymore. My professional aspirations were long gone, and all of this money was being wasted, yet I shared how I felt with no one.

After a miserable performance in the first round, I lied to my mom and told her I was sick and having severe stomach pain and couldn't play. So I withdrew from the tournament, and we were on a flight home the next day. It makes me sad to write these words today. I would love to be back at that tournament with my mom, even if I shot a million. Instead of talking to her about it, I bottled all of it up inside. That was my coping mechanism. I was so worried about letting them down, and everyone seeing me as a failure, including myself.

I brushed off my on-course struggles by saying I was just a little burned out, needed some time to rest, and would be ready to go in the fall at college. As mentioned earlier, Arkansas didn't have a women's golf team at the time, so I had to look elsewhere even though I didn't want to leave home. I now understand that my food and body obsessions significantly affected my social skills back then, too. I could fake it when necessary, but all I wanted to do when I wasn't working out was be at home. Other than the gym, it was my only safe space.

Despite being recruited by nearly every top golf program in the country, I signed a letter of intent to play college golf at Southern Methodist because my good friend, Annie Deets, was there. Annie was a year older than me and one of my closest friends in junior golf. During her freshman year at SMU, she did what typical first-year college students do. She socialized, made new friends, and joined a sorority. I had no interest in any of that. I went to class, golf practice, and the dining room downstairs for every meal, and that was it. The rest of the time I spent in my dorm room. I was miserable and homesick. Only now, I wasn't working out but still had my food obsession, which had metastasized into a full-blown phobia because I wasn't exercising. My biggest fear had become a real possibility. I was scared to death of getting fat. While the dire state of depression had begun to kick in, I had no idea of the difficult road ahead.

At this point, I thought all I needed was a change of scenery. *SMU must not be the place for me, and that's why I'm feeling this way,* I kept telling myself. Since I was so homesick, I knew I only had two options. I could quit golf and move back home or contact the coach at Tulsa University, which was only a two-hour drive from my hometown, to find out if the full scholarship offer was still available if I decided to transfer.

Dale McNamara was a legendary women's college golf coach, as was her program. During Dale's tenure, she led Tulsa to four NCAA titles, eventually earning her a spot in the National Collegiate Golf Hall of Fame. To my delight (and surprise), when I reached out that day, she was genuinely glad to hear from me. Dale had recruited me vigorously during my high school years and didn't hide her disappointment when I decided to sign with SMU instead of Tulsa. It was a hard decision because I knew I'd let her down. Within a day of explaining my situation at SMU, she called back and said the scholarship was still available, and I felt this overwhelming wave of happiness for the first time in a long time. But it didn't take long for the feeling of joy to start fading away.

I remember that day in the car, driving home after the first semester at SMU with my bags packed and Dallas in the rearview mirror. Everything was going to be great, I thought, until all of a sudden, it wasn't. Once the Christmas break started to wind down, the realization that I had to leave home for another school to play golf began to set in. I didn't want to play golf anymore. I didn't even want to go to class or see anyone. It was a horrible place to be while everyone else my age seemed to be having the time of their lives. I was just 18 years old and already experiencing what felt like a painful divorce—not just from the sport I'd played most of my life, but from the sense of self-worth I'd built around it.

CHAPTER 6

MONSTER

UNLIKE AT SMU, I had my own dorm room at Tulsa. It was small, outdated, and without a fraction of warmth whatsoever. My mom did her best to brighten it up, but the energy just wasn't there. I'm sure where I was at this point in my life emotionally had a lot to do with the staleness that surrounded me. I don't remember much about golf or my classes (many of which I rarely attended), but I do remember the shared bathroom very well. A few weeks into my new life at Tulsa University, still doing my best not to eat anything with fat in it, I was in my dorm room one night devouring these little low-calorie animal-shaped cinnamon crackers. Then, all of a sudden, I freaked out after realizing that I'd almost eaten the entire box. Feeling an enormous amount of guilt and fearing it would make my clothes not fit the next day, I walked into the shared bathroom and was relieved to discover that no one else was in there. That was the first time I made myself throw up.

Anyone who's suffered from bulimia will tell you that you get really good at making yourself regurgitate. I don't want to go into all the horrible details because it'd be hard to write about and even more uncomfortable for you to read. But that day in the bathroom unleashed what would become a horrible cycle of binging and purging. I learned the types of foods I could easily throw up and tried to avoid those that made it more difficult. I had the entire process down to a science. It usually didn't happen after meals, although it sometimes did if I indulged in certain forbidden foods—especially heavy carbs and desserts. Ice cream was my go-to when I felt the urge, as were certain types of cereals and cakes. Foods I'd denied myself for years because of their fat, calorie, and sugar content suddenly became my outlet. Instead of talking about my problems with family or friends, I ate. And then I purged in secrecy where no one could stop me or control it because no one knew about it. If I was home at my parent's house, I would tell them I was taking a shower when I needed to make myself throw up. That way, the running water would disguise the obscene sound my body was making in defiance. Surprisingly, no one had any idea about my agonizing secret. That's how good I was at hiding it.

Inconceivably, binging and purging gave me a sense of power because it was one of the few things in my life that I could fully control. It was mine and mine alone. I made the choices, no one else. But, as I would later learn in therapy, that's how eating disorders thrive. Your secrecy actually gives *it* power, not the other way around. I was the powerless victim in this horrible cycle of harming myself.

Bulimia has a punishing effect on the body. You can become vitamin deficient and suffer from weakness and dizzy spells, headaches, and constipation. These were all too familiar side effects for me. Strangely enough, I actually gained about 25 pounds, which made me want to binge and purge even more. Our bodies are smart, and mine was holding onto every calorie it could out of fear I would eliminate it on my own, without giving it any say-so. My body, unfortunately, was right.

This monster ruled my life for eight unforgiving years until I finally decided to get help. Desperate and miserable, I mustered up the courage to confide in a friend who connected me with a therapist she knew who specialized in eating disorders. To this day, I still say Teri Haskins saved my life.

CHAPTER 7

FACING THE DEMONS

THE HARDEST PART of writing this memoir has been opening up about all aspects of my life, which I'm not very comfortable doing. I was raised in a fairly conservative town with parents who,
excluding politics, were pretty conservative as well. I blame that on
their religious affiliations growing up.

Not long after I started high school, I knew something wasn't quite
right. Even though I was dating boys, any physical attraction I had
to them in the beginning quickly faded, and I lost interest. I always
played it off as just being picky. But when I finally realized at the age
of 20 that those feelings didn't go away with girls the way they did
with boys, my life morphed into an emotional pendulum, swinging
back and forth between "sinning" and knee-jerk guilt.

The realization that I was gay (a word I'm still not entirely comfortable with, probably because of its lingering stereotypes) and that
my family would likely never approve of it made my initial attempts at
dating insanely tough to process. In many ways, staying in the closet
felt like a hopelessly miserable future existence. But on the flip side,
having my family disown me and going to hell seemed much worse.

Even though my parents had always taught me to be honest, I knew that keeping my sexuality a secret was a clear exception to this rule.

Life was hard and only seemed to be getting harder. I was embarrassed to tell anyone I was attracted to women. I had an eating disorder. And I'd completely lost my love for playing competitive golf, the one thing I knew people would still admire me for. To put it bluntly, I was a total *fucking* train wreck.

After three painful years of bouncing around to three different colleges, everyone seemed *so proud* when I became the first scholarship player for the newly formed women's golf program at the University of Arkansas one year after leaving Tulsa. Then I disappointed those very same people when I announced, after playing for just one year, that I was quitting. I walked away from my dreams of winning major championships on the LPGA Tour and never looked back. I was done—this time for good.

Reflecting on it now, I'm sure that my secret struggles with bulimia and my other secret life were key psychological sticking points that had some subconscious connection to my divorce from golf. After I walked away from the team, I became even more depressed than I was before. When I felt scared or stressed, or self-conscious about my body, I would binge on junk food for a false sense of comfort. Then, after the inevitable crash, I would feel ashamed and throw it back up as punishment for my transgressions.

I finally reached a breaking point during my mid-twenties and decided to get help. I was miserable and scared of what was happening to my life and to my body. To this day, it's still hard to relive those moments of binging and purging in my head. I want to talk to that young woman and help her. Thankfully, a therapist named Teri Haskins became my saving grace. She helped me understand the vicious cycle that dragged on from my first year of college into my late twenties and, most importantly, why letting go of the secrecy of it was my salvation.

I worked a job waiting tables in Little Rock to finish school and pay for the sessions instead of asking anyone for money and risking exposure. Teri and I spent a significant amount of time unraveling my mental chaos. I began to realize that much of the reason for the food abuse was wrapped up in the shame I felt about being gay. I wanted to be okay with myself and have my parents love and respect me regardless of my sexual orientation. But I also knew how narrow-minded much of society still was about people like me back then, too. It took a while for my life to improve—years, in fact. In hindsight, getting a therapist is one of the best decisions I've ever made. Honestly, it may be the best. But it was also the hardest decision I ever made, too. Admitting you need help isn't easy. In time, though, I learned to love myself again even though I no longer loved golf. Therapy taught me that I wasn't a failure. I was human.

I can't fully explain why I suffered from bulimia, although it does make a lot more sense now. Years of intense therapy will give you some pretty clear answers. Every Wednesday, I'd meet Teri and talk for 50 minutes in her office. She had this perfectly placed fuzzy purple pillow on her sofa that became my companion during our weekly sessions. When she asked questions I didn't want to answer, I clung to that stuffed safety net as tight as I possibly could. Those first several sessions were agonizing. I'd built this fortress around my life emotionally and had a hard time opening up. It made me feel vulnerable and weak. To disguise my discomfort, I tried discussing other topics to take up the time because I was too embarrassed and ashamed to talk about what mattered. Teri would let me stray for a moment but always found a way to redirect the conversation.

It's worth mentioning here that I recently learned that being embarrassed and ashamed are two entirely different emotions. "Embarrassed" has to do with what others think of you, while being "ashamed" is what you think of yourself. In the early days of sitting in Teri's office, I'm pretty sure I was both.

Teri was a perfect fit for me because she didn't talk much. Instead, she asked important questions and listened, which forced me to open up—something I'd become very skilled at avoiding all those years. By getting me to talk, she allowed me to break down my walls, as painful as it was. I thrived on secrecy, and now this woman I was paying was subtly forcing me to knock down those barriers one session at a time. Eventually, it made me feel safe and I learned to trust her more than I ever thought I could.

After a few months of seeing Teri, she told me about a weekly group therapy session where other people with eating disorders got together and would talk about their experiences. I immediately blew off that idea. This wasn't something I'd ever consider, I told myself, and I told her it wasn't for me. Not a chance in hell. But the more comfortable I became opening up about my life, the more I realized this was *exactly* what I needed to keep getting better.

I haven't binged and purged since my late twenties, but I often think about those days and welcome any opportunity to share them with others. With mental health awareness at an all-time high, I'm quick to tell my story, hoping it might make someone else feel safe to tell their story. What we go through matters—the good and the bad. I understand now that by remaining silent all those years and doing my best not to let anyone down, the only person I truly let down was myself.

While I may not be proud of the actual eating disorder, I am proud of the courage and determination it took to free myself from those demons. I wouldn't change what I went through for anything because it played such a significant role in the person I am today. I want people to know that it's okay to not be okay—that it's okay to ask for help. There shouldn't be a stigma with going to therapy. It should be encouraged and talked about more. God knows this world needs more therapists in it. There's not only a mental health crisis brewing but there's also a crisis surrounding a lack of resources to help.

If you're in a place similar to where I was all those years ago, I encourage you to find someone to talk to—even if it's just a friend at first. Being vulnerable isn't a sign of weakness. It's a sign of strength and the only avenue that fully allows the healing process to begin. Embarrassment, shame, and secrecy are the enemies. It takes time to let those things go, but once you do, your life will change forever.

The self-acceptance and mental fortitude I gained after going through therapy in my late twenties proved invaluable when it came time for me to tell my story about what I experienced at Golf Channel. By undoing years of learned people-pleasing behavior, I was—unknowingly at the time—teaching myself how to become a "troublemaker" and stand up for those who needed it, including myself.

PART II

LIGHTS, CAMERA, ACTION

CHAPTER 8

TV LIFE

ONCE MY PROFESSIONAL golf aspirations were gone for good, I realized that I had absolutely no idea what I wanted to do for a living. I got my undergrad degree in pre-law before deciding at the very end that I didn't want to be a lawyer. Out of desperation, I tried phone sales and failed miserably. Nothing in the Help Wanted section of the newspaper came close to piquing my interest. So I ended up going back to the restaurant where I waited tables while finishing my degree and became a manager. I liked the job and, more importantly, I liked the people even more. It was a familiar place where I could be myself, even though it didn't offer a great future. I wasn't making much money, and deep down, I knew there was much more I was supposed to be doing.

Eventually, I discovered live television, and my eyes were opened wide. I had a couple of friends who worked at the local NBC affiliate in Little Rock, and being around them doing their jobs was a blast. It reminded me of the adrenaline rush that playing competitive sports offered, which I missed more than I realized. It didn't take long before I returned to school to get a minor in broadcast journalism.

One year later, I landed my first job as a sports anchor/reporter in Columbus, Mississippi. My family thought I was crazy to take such a sizable pay cut—only making $18,000—and move to a small town where I knew no one to do a job I wasn't fully prepared to do. I'd gone from a world where I was a relative expert at my craft to venturing into a media landscape that was entirely foreign to me. I also had to borrow $10,000 from my cousin Allison to be able to afford the only one-bedroom apartment within the town's city limits which didn't make me feel like I was in college again.

I spent 13 months at WCBI-TV in Columbus and loved every minute of it even though, at the age of 30, I was basically making minimum wage. I loved attending high school football games, Ole Miss baseball games, and Mississippi State basketball games. I couldn't believe I was getting paid, albeit not very much, to cover sports for a living. It didn't take long before I started setting my sights even higher.

Before I knew it, I was hired by a much larger station in Cincinnati, Ohio, to do a job I quickly realized, once again, that I was neither prepared nor qualified to have at the time. I can guarantee if my eventual boss, John Popovich, had asked me to do a live audition the day I came up for the interview, he wouldn't have offered me the job. I was in no way ready for that position. It was one of those moments, being so new to the business, where the only way to learn was by being thrown into the fire. Thankfully, I've always had a relentless attitude when I set my sights on what I want.

One particularly pressure-packed memory from that job comes to mind. I was a big baseball fan as a kid—my dad and I watched the Cubs play on WGN almost every night during baseball season. Fast-forward to me standing on a major league field, covering the Cincinnati Reds, about to report live for the first time. I remember being so overwhelmed by the magnitude of the moment that I couldn't fully appreciate how cool it was to be there. The Reds were hosting the Pirates at Great American Ballpark, and I was a nervous wreck.

I'd only worked in television for 13 months and had probably only done three actual live reports during that time.

The station where I worked in Columbus typically had us pre-tape our reports five to ten minutes ahead of time because the TV trucks and satellite feeds weren't reliable enough to carry them live. As a result, the first time I reported live for the Reds, down on the field, was a near-disaster. Once the red light on the camera came on and the anchor set me up for the hit, I was so rattled by the enormity of the situation I barely kept from hyperventilating and could feel my knees starting to buckle. I even remember my cameraman, Mark Slaughter, asking me afterward, "Were you just nervous, or what? Look, we have to make this better, or you aren't going to last long here."

The most unnerving part was that although I'd done my research and knew what I was talking about, I still felt unable to properly convey the information on live television. While some may assume that proper preparation is all a person needs in those high-pressure situations, there was no way I, or anyone else, could be fully ready to sit on that hot seat unless they had one thing: experience. Needless to say, I was very green. In many ways, it's similar to a basketball player preparing at home to hit a game-winning free throw or a golfer trying to simulate having a 15-footer to win a major. You simply can't replicate those moments, no matter how hard you try to visualize yourself in the situation.

As embarrassing as that first live report was, I managed to make it through the rest of the evening unscathed. Still, I felt completely in over my head, facing the daunting realization that I might very well fail miserably—or somehow figure things out and make them work to my advantage. I knew I had to get better, fast. But I also realized the more pressure I put on myself, the worse it might get.

I finally learned the way to improve my live reports in the beginning was to make them shorter and more straightforward and, if a soundbite was involved, to get to it quicker. Over time, this taught me how to stay cool on-air and alleviate the pressure. I also sought as much advice as possible from the seasoned veterans I worked with at WCPO. The generosity they gave with their time and insight was crucial to my development.

After Cincinnati, I headed to Knoxville, Tennessee. It was a smaller market, but the job was in news as a morning show host, which meant it was a higher-profile position and paid almost twice as much. Eventually, though, I realized I missed being in the sports side of the business, so when an opportunity came to work at the Big Ten Network in Chicago as a reporter/studio host/play-by-play announcer, I jumped all over it.

––––––––––––

Throughout my TV career, I've battled anxiety issues on-air. There were many more moments in Cincinnati besides that first live report where I didn't know if I could make it through the hit. When it happens, you feel like you're suffocating. Anyone who's ever been in this situation knows how claustrophobic it can be. It didn't happen all the time, but it happened often enough that I constantly feared it. I tried breathing exercises, meditation, lorazepam—anything that could potentially ease the problem. I can't speak for everyone who's suffered from this type of performance anxiety, but for me, it seemed to be a confidence issue. As time passed and I became more comfortable in my job and my ability to perform, it happened less and less. I'm fortunate in that regard because it's not always so simple. Anxiety is powerful and can be debilitating. It's negatively impacted the careers of some of the best athletes and entertainers in the world.

When some of the same anxiety issues I experienced in Cincinnati started to rear their ugly head again during my first year at Golf Channel, I discovered a book by Dan Harris called *Ten Percent Happier*, where the former *Good Morning America* co-anchor wrote in great detail about the panic attacks he used to suffer from on-air. Reading about someone at his level in the business who seemed to battle a more intense form of anxiety than I did helped me better understand what I was going through. It also taught me not to be so hard on myself, which I've tried to carry over to all aspects of my life.

CHAPTER 9

DREAM JOB

---

*A dream job is a position that combines an activity, skill, or passion with
a money-making opportunity.*

—Jamie Birt, Indeed

AFTER GRINDING MY WAY through the television sports
world with jobs in Mississippi, Tennessee, Ohio, and eventually the Big Ten Network, I questioned whether I wanted to continue
in this business. I'd moved around quite a bit the past several years,
trying to climb the ladder. Plus, I missed seeing my family and still
wasn't making very much money. And even though I had a deep
passion for all sports as far back as I can remember, I couldn't shake
the feeling that this wasn't what I was supposed to be doing.

In 2011, I decided to break away from the traditional sports
broadcast domain and try my own thing. Streaming shows were still
relatively unheard of at the time. But I'd been around enough forward-
thinking people in the industry who believed that the entire television
landscape would soon go in that direction, so I launched an internet

show called *SEC Press Pass* a couple of years before the creation of the SEC Network.

We were starting to gain some traction when I reached out via email to an on-air talent agent in New York named Gregg Willinger. I told Gregg that I might be interested in trying to find some freelance opportunities if he'd be interested in representing me. After all, I still had bills to pay. He responded by asking me to send him my demo reel (which I did immediately), and he called me within hours. After a quick hello, the first words out of his mouth were, "Lisa, can I ask why in the world you aren't still working in TV?" I didn't know how to explain to a complete stranger where I was with it all mentally, so I told him I just needed a break, which he accepted without much interrogation.

A few weeks later, I signed a contract with Gregg and patiently waited for the right opportunity to come around while still trying to grow *SEC Press Pass*. After a few months had passed, and on the heels of a couple of uninteresting possibilities, he called about a potential opening at Golf Channel. I could tell he was exhilarated to deliver the news, while I'm sure he could tell that I was oddly on the fence.

After everything that had happened, the chance to re-enter golf in a completely different way put me at somewhat of a crossroads. I'd started to play a lot again—not competitively, but regularly with my good friends Ed and Zac David in Little Rock, which is why the chance to work at Golf Channel caused this deep, internal turmoil. I was so scared of losing the passion I'd only recently rediscovered for something that used to mean everything in the world to me to chase a job in an industry that I wasn't even sure I still wanted to be in. So I asked Gregg if he could give me a few days to think about it. He seemed a bit confused but, again, didn't press too hard.

After talking it over with my family and friends, I eventually (but still somewhat reluctantly) told him I was interested in pursuing it. A couple of weeks later, he said in an email that the executive producer,

Molly Solomon, would reach out. *Wait, what?* I thought. *The executive producer is a woman?* I'd been in sports television for a decade, and in all those years, I never had a female co-worker in my department, let alone a female boss. I couldn't have been more excited to hear this news.

On February 14, 2013, I received the following email from Molly:

> Lisa,
> I asked Gregg if I could reach out to you directly. Would love to talk to you at some point.
> Let me know what day/time works.
> Sincerely,
> Molly

It was simple and to the point, but my eyes lit up when I read it. She said she would *love* to talk to me, which seemed much more genuine and less intimidating than any other email I'd ever received from a potential boss. I couldn't wait to have our first conversation.

To be honest, I don't remember much about the initial call other than it was brief. From my experience, Molly's never been one to get too in-depth. However, I didn't learn that about her until much later. When things didn't progress as quickly as I'd hoped in the beginning, I wondered, *Did I say something wrong or not say enough during the call?* These are the types of questions that over-analyzers (like me) typically ask themselves. The entire process was a lesson in patience, which isn't my strong suit. In Molly's defense, and I won't say that often, it was during the time of year when golf transforms from a quick jog to a full-on sprint—meaning the major championship season was about to kick off.

In a week or so, she sent another email inviting me to come to Orlando on March 11 for a visit and audition. By all accounts, the trip went as well as could be expected, and six weeks later, I was back for a follow-up visit and second audition.

My initial read on Molly was that everything about her seemed positive, upbeat, energetic, and vibrant. While I never expected the possibility of working at a national network to be easy, the thought of having a female executive producer who would surely understand the challenges we sometimes face as women made it a hell of a lot more appealing. Because of this, I wanted the job more than I ever expected I would. Finally, on September 10, 2013, I signed a three-year contract with Golf Channel that would change my life forever.

CHAPTER 10

THE BOYS' CLUB

J**ANUARY 1, 2014.** My first official day at Golf Channel. I was being introduced during a segment on *Morning Drive*. Even though I'd had plenty of live television experience by now, as I mentioned before, I still experienced occasional bouts of anxiety. On this particular day, I felt like I was going to throw up.

Gary Williams was hosting the show and couldn't have made me feel more welcome. I'll always remember how encouraging he was while I was on the verge of passing out. I'm pretty sure my nervousness showed up during the interview because the people who are closest to me said afterward that it was great, but they could also tell I was slightly nervous. I think they were being kind using the word "slightly." To this day, I've never watched the interview because, to be honest, I don't like watching myself on TV.

Most of the people at Golf Channel were just like Gary—team players who'd do anything to help you succeed. Then there were the others, a small group of entitled antagonists who sadly made this book possible. Many companies today, because they understand the importance of respect in the workplace, have an unwritten rule regarding these types of employees. I call it the no-asshole policy. Not only did Golf Channel not protect its people from this type of destructive behavior, it often encouraged it. Like a lot of places, that group at the network was well known and had a very familiar name: "the Boys' Club."

My first real encounter with anyone in this group happened a few months into my job. As most of us do, especially early on, I was grinding every day in my new role. Whatever they asked me to do, I did. When I wasn't working at Golf Channel, I was watching Golf Channel. It was an obsession. Finally, after working every day for a few weeks straight, I headed to the beach to spend some time with a family member who was vacationing there to recharge my batteries. I was exhausted—mentally and physically. Less than an hour after I arrived, I got a call from Mark Summer saying he'd somehow messed up the schedule and needed me to come in. He told me he didn't have any other options. I was demoralized knowing that, as the new person, I couldn't say no. So I drove back home, quickly changed, and hustled into work. Not long after I arrived, I was walking back to my desk from the bathroom and heard the lead producer that day on the phone laughing with someone on the other end about how I had to drive an hour back from the beach on my only day off because Mark screwed up the schedule. He continued to laugh while saying I wasn't happy about it. It wasn't the laughing that put me over the edge; it was the obvious satisfaction he seemed to be taking from my misery.

As I approached him, I couldn't help myself. "Why would you laugh at something like that?" I asked. He quickly turned pale, realizing I'd overheard his mockery of me. "I don't know how this is funny at all."

He tried to backpedal, saying he was laughing about Mark making a mistake and that it had nothing to do with me. I looked at him and didn't say another word, but what I really wanted to do was let him have it. If you mess up, just own it and apologize, and all can be forgiven. Instead, he was trying to cover up his behavior.

I'm well aware that the good ol' boys' club doesn't like women like me. They can't control us very easily, and we're virtually branded as "troublemakers" whenever we challenge them. From that day forward, this group of guys basically treated me like an outsider…and, to be honest, I was perfectly fine with it.

———

Boys' clubs like the one at Golf Channel are rampant throughout the business world. According to most professionals I know, there are pockets of them everywhere—from the executive offices to the mail room. They start innocently enough, bonding over shared interests like sports or weekend festivities. These activities on their own aren't the problem. It's when they start making backdoor deals on the golf course or at the bar and consistently give these same buddies advantages or amenities at work. That's when this type of behavior becomes unfair.

Besides women, marginalized groups also suffer because of these boys' clubs. For starters, it sets the tone in a corporate environment that all too often anyone who isn't a white, connected man isn't recognized as respectable by the powers that be. That false impression lingers in these employees' thoughts and does nothing to help them persevere in the workplace either.

The boys' clubs are also a way to wield power and keep other people quiet. As cited in the *Washington Post* article that exposed this systemic culture, which you'll read about in great detail later, there were women at Golf Channel who wanted to have speakers come in to teach them how to negotiate for equal pay. According to Ben Strauss' reporting, the network made significant strides to quash these speakers from meeting with female employees. Even worse, they passed off the responsibility for delivering this news to HR manager Julie Lusk.

As you'll soon learn, much like Molly Solomon, Julie Lusk was another all-too-convenient female flak jacket for the network whenever HR became involved.

Julie and Molly's betrayal of women is nothing new. For years, women who reached positions of power had to act like men to get ahead. The worst part about powerful women aligning with these boys' clubs is that it doesn't truly help their cause either. They're perceived as weak, malleable pawns who can be made to do whatever the male management wants while simultaneously setting their female co-workers back.

Their behavior can only be defined one way: weak. They're complicit in their crimes by being unwilling to help break up male-dominant work environments. Without accountability, this type of gender betrayal will remain persistent.

Unfortunately, most people seem to want to fit in with the mainstream culture, especially at work. Since being a woman already makes us virtual outsiders to begin with, it starts to feel like many would be willing to do anything to break the ice with our male superiors. Sadly, this borderline desperation only encourages people to compromise their ethics and morals to do so. At that point, the underrepresented stop bridging any potential social gaps and merely obstruct the path for their successors.

A friend of mine holds a master's degree in organizational development and worked in human resources at a Fortune 500 company for more than a decade. During a recent discussion we had on this topic, she made that exact point in the most perfectly succinct way: "I think there are a lot of women who've had to scrape and bite and claw their way to the top, but in doing so they've left their soul behind."

Businesses are driven by their bottom line. Companies, unfortunately, often seem to value profit over treating their employees fairly. When someone claims she's the victim of sexism in the workplace, she's often met with some form of, "You have to be tough and grow a thick skin if you want to survive in this environment." This tired cliché has been the blanket stereotype that keeps people in the boys' club warm at night. Sure, we must all learn to be tough in business, but part of that toughness requires calling out discriminatory behavior when we see it.

CHAPTER 11

RELATIONSHIPS AND RETALIATION

THE YEAR AFTER I began my job at Golf Channel as a studio host, a young woman named Angela Akins was hired to be a live tournament reporter. Angela and I didn't work together too often in the beginning, and because she split time between Orlando and Austin—where her then-husband still lived—we didn't initially develop a very close friendship.

Angela's an incredibly nice, good-hearted person. I realized this almost immediately the first time we met. Not only was she good at her job and worked hard to get to this level in the sports broadcasting industry, but she also had strong credentials in golf to back it up. Angela grew up playing the game competitively in her home state of Texas, eventually earning a scholarship to play collegiately at the University of Texas. It was nice to have another female on-air talent in the newsroom who knew the game as well as she did.

Later that year, she told me about some issues she was having at home. The time apart from her husband was starting to take its toll on both of them. And to make matters more complicated, Molly had been on her to get a permanent residence in Orlando, which seemed unnecessary to me. Most of Angela's job was spent on the road, which should've allowed her to live anywhere. I'm sure this pressure only added to the strain on her marriage.

Angela and her first husband would eventually divorce, and a very well-known PGA Tour player asked her out a while later. No one in my circle at work knew about this, including me, but it didn't take long for the office gossip to start running rampant. If there was anyone who didn't deserve this kind of behind-your-back mockery, it was Angela.

Once Molly got wind of it, she started asking a lot of questions to all of us. One afternoon, while I was preparing for that night's *Golf Central*, she asked me to come into her office for a few minutes. I had a pretty good idea what it was about. Molly had a way of asking these types of awkward questions in a valley girl, aw-shucks sort of way. She said something like: *Hey, rumors are starting to fly about Angela and Sergio. I just can't believe it. Why would she do something like this and jeopardize her career? I mean, she has such a bright future ahead of her. Do you know anything about it?* Her tone was weird.

When all the talk began about Angela seeing Sergio Garcia, the long-timers in the newsroom immediately started questioning whether she'd get fired, which made absolutely zero sense to me. Even though Sergio has been one of the biggest names in golf for the last 20 years or so, that's still no reason to fire her.

Without hesitation, I told Molly I knew nothing about Angela and Sergio, which was honest. Then she carried on and on in detail about how if Angela had just been forthcoming and hadn't hidden it from her, this wouldn't be as big of an issue—that she could've found a way to figure something out.

Now I was perplexed. Did Molly care about Angela seeing a Tour player, Angela seeing this *particular* Tour player, or the fact that she wasn't in the loop? At that moment, it felt like the latter. She kept talking about the importance of maintaining our journalistic integrity, and all I could think to myself was, *We're covering golf here, not invading Normandy.* Besides, Molly and Geoff were two executives who were married and working together. Doesn't that violate workplace integrity? To say it seemed hypocritical is a monumental understatement.

Not long after Molly's pseudo interrogation in her office, Angela took me to see her new apartment, which wasn't very far from our Golf Channel studios. I told her there were some rumblings about her and Sergio and thought it'd be best for her not to give me any insight because I was being asked about it by the higher-ups. I told her my only advice was to be as upfront as possible with anyone in authority at the network who asked because that seemed to be their focus, as ridiculous as it sounded.

I felt awful for her. People kept saying how Sergio had this rocky past with women. He would keep relationships as long as they benefited him and then leave them in a flash. Everyone I heard gossiping about it at Golf Channel predicted it would be the same scenario for Angela—they'd see each other for a short time, she'd lose her job, and he'd be off to the next one. I couldn't have been happier when Sergio won the Masters with his fiancée by his side. They're now happily married with two children and have never looked back. Ironically, Golf Channel ended up treating Angela the way the naysayers at the network predicted Sergio would treat her.

Not surprisingly, Angela's contract wasn't renewed at the end of the year, and soon after Sergio's major championship triumph, she gave the following interview to ESPN's Jason Sobel regarding her ouster from Golf Channel:

> Garcia, whose personal life has often been tabloid fodder over the years, simply answered her questions in front of a television camera, and that was that.

"There was nothing [romantic]," he says now. "Nothing for a while."

Over the next few months, they would become friendly on a professional level. Every so often, Garcia would post a low round, and Akins would be there to interview him afterward. But according to her, it wasn't until early 2016 that he finally asked her out.

All of which, she says, led to a weighty decision:

She felt like she had to choose between her career and Garcia.

"I did feel that, because I was forced to feel that way," she says.

Akins maintains that there were no provisions in her contract that would prohibit her from having a relationship with a player.

"Nothing was ever in writing. Believe me, I checked. I read everything that I signed."

According to a Golf Channel spokesperson, the company has a long-standing policy which states reporters are not allowed to date players on tours they cover.

"If it had been up to me, I would have continued to do what I was doing and found a way to make it work and just test the waters, but that's not how it worked out," she says. "That wasn't the opportunity that I was given, and I accept that. I had a wonderful time when I was at Golf Channel.... I think it's amazing how everything works out. I made all those great friends, and now I still get to see them, just in a different role."

In the months that followed, her dismissal led to all sorts of unprofessional behavior. My day-to-day boss, Mark Summer, was so furious that she didn't tell him about her relationship with Sergio that it became an everyday frivolous conversation inside the building. He was obsessed with it. One day when I got to work, someone had printed and taped at least 25 8 x 11 images all over his office of Angela and Sergio hugging after he won the Masters just to get under Mark's skin, and it worked. It was one of several times to come that I was embarrassed by what was taking place at the network I once admired.

Little did I know then just how much Angela and Sergio's relationship would affect my future status at Golf Channel. The following year, out of concern for my own job, I had to disclose a relationship that opened my eyes to the people I reported to at the network. Looking back, it was not only an extremely personal violation—it crossed the legal bounds of employment law. And not surprisingly, Molly and Geoff were the people who allowed it to happen.

CHAPTER 12

THE B-TEAM

WHILE MUCH OF THIS BOOK details the many transgressions that occurred during my time at Golf Channel, there's a much longer list of great memories I'll always cherish from those seven years. It's why I stayed as long as I did and why it was so hard to say goodbye. Many of the people I adored the most were part of what we jokingly, but affectionately, called the B-Team.

When I came back for the second audition in 2013, my nerves were through the roof because I knew I had a good shot at getting the job. Otherwise, there wouldn't have been a second audition. Within a couple hours of being at the network for round two, I was back in Studio-A and ready to go. Only this time, the experience was much different.

Studio-A was an impressive setup. I'd been in several network-level operations throughout my career, and this was, by far, the most expansive and versatile of them all. We had a main studio desk that could fit three people comfortably and four wide, if necessary. There was also a floating desk for two people (typically an analyst and a host) that we used most of the time for our Monday through Wednesday

Golf Central shows, which was my primary role. Since the desk was floating, multiple backdrops could be created to make the studio appear larger. There was a putting green and hitting bay side-by-side where we did single camera stand-ups to introduce features and instructional segments throughout the show. Then there was what I referred to as the lounge—a sitting area, slightly elevated with relaxed living-room-style chairs.

This massive space, which was always freezing cold and full of bright lights, would eventually feel like home. This day, however, it was intimidating beyond belief. After reviewing all the highlights, writing my scripts, and going through the hour-or-so-long hair and make-up process, it was finally time for the most important audition of my life. I was sitting behind the anchor desk with the lights on full blast. The crew was spread out across the studio—three guys operating cameras, a floor director, an audio person, and a couple of extra people just in case. I had my IFB (earpiece) in, waiting to get the instructions from the producer while desperately trying not to show that my hands and knees were shaking. Then, all of a sudden, a familiar sound started playing in my ear: *Hit that line, hit that line, keep on going...Move that ball right down the field! Give a cheer. Rah, rah! Never fear. Rah, rah! Arkansas will never yield...*

I couldn't believe it. The "University of Arkansas Fight Song" started playing unannounced, and it changed my entire mood. I could feel this massive grin come across my face, and when I looked up, I noticed that everyone in the studio was smiling along with me. They all started giving me thumbs-up signals and were saying things like, "Let's go, Razorback!" and "C'mon, Lisa!" clearly rooting for me to knock it out of the park. I was blown away by their reaction. These strangers were supporting me as though we were great friends with a strong connection already. I can't begin to tell you how much that meant to me that day and the confidence it gave me to do well—not just for me, but for them, too.

Over the years, the crew would become like family. No matter what happened at work or what kind of mood I was in, they made everything better anytime I was in that studio, even when the shows didn't go as planned. They were vocal and encouraging in a way that endeared me to them forever.

It wasn't just the studio crew, either. Golf Channel was home to so many incredible people in every department. We talked in the break rooms, in the hallways, upstairs in the cafe, in the edit suites, in the bathrooms, by the copy machine—you name it. When Comcast/NBCUniversal decided to move its Golf Channel operations to Stamford, Connecticut, where NBC Sports is based, many of these people lost their dream jobs, too. Devastated doesn't even begin to describe the grief they felt—many of whom had spent their entire careers working at the network.

To quote a *Golfweek* article that was published on June 22, 2020, "The Golf Channel on Monday told most of its Orlando-based staff that it would be laid off starting August 29, then allowed those staffers to reapply for a smaller pool of jobs."

As described, those layoffs began on August 29...and the very next day, rather than showing remorse for the people who'd just been shown the door, Molly Solomon was celebrating publicly on Twitter. You see, this highly paid executive, who seems to have everlasting job security, had just broken 80 on the golf course for the first time:

> Never EVER give up. 25 years after I took up the game...
> Today was the finish I dreamed of. Birdie at the last to
> break 80. Thank you @martinhallGC. Thank you forever
> golf partner @GeoffRussellGC

I believe that tells you all you need to know about Molly Solomon.

———————

Two months after finding out my own fate at Golf Channel—that I was being demoted to a part-time reporter the following year and would no longer work in the studio—my final day hosting *Golf Central* had arrived. I'd been on edge about this particular show since the news was delivered.

I was in the makeup room, which was my refuge in the building. Those women were like sisters. We laughed, cried, told crazy stories, and planned our future escapades. You name it; it probably happened in there. And, just like Vegas, it stayed in there, too.

I purposely didn't wear mascara to work that day, knowing I'd tear up at least a dozen times. But now, I had to gather myself because there was one final show to do. Thank God I went into the makeup room early that day because it took a while to regain my composure after what I saw. There were cards taped all over the mirrors, fresh flowers, balloons, signs, and 10–15 miniature bottles of Johnnie Walker Black—my go-to. The make-up crew, the studio crew...they all wanted to make sure I felt their love. I did, and still do to this day.

Despite all the fury and frustration over the years, what upsets me most is how Golf Channel and NBCUniversal's lawyers still try to characterize my demotion, then the non-renewal, simply as cutting back during the move from Orlando to Stamford, Connecticut. Besides all the reasons laid out in this book, the most obvious way to debunk their assertion is by looking at which positions were mostly let go during the layoffs.

Like most TV networks, when budget cuts happen, the behind-the-scenes staff, sadly, are the folks who end up losing their jobs. Rarely do the on-air personalities get laid off. Golf Channel phased out four of us during this time, two of whom (both males) were offered positions in Connecticut, only to have those offers rescinded for reasons from what I've been told the network considered to be contract violations. The only two on-air people who were let go simply for "budgetary" reasons were Chantel McCabe and me. Like me,

Chantel stood up for herself. And, also like me, one of Golf Channel's lead analysts, Brandel Chamblee, had a beef with her. The man who's famous for blocking people on Twitter once blocked her over something so meaningless, you'd roll your eyes.

There are many reasons why behavior like this needs to be exposed, mainly because companies often cite "budget" when they want to get rid of people they deem to be inconvenient who haven't done anything that warrants being fired. I'm sure many people have seen similar actions at their workplace. The only way to stop them from doing this is to shine a bright light on these situations. Otherwise, plenty of good people will continue to unfairly lose their jobs.

PART III

TROUBLE IN PARADISE

CHAPTER 13

CHAMBLEE

IF YOU WATCH golf, you probably know the name Brandel
Chamblee. If you aren't a golf fan, I'm sure you know plenty of
people just like him. Brandel grew up to be a good golfer, and after
graduating from the University of Texas, he went on to win one tournament on the PGA Tour in his 18-year professional career—the
Greater Vancouver Open.

In 2003, Brandel lost his PGA Tour card and was hired by Golf
Channel as a lead analyst. By all accounts, he's a well-known student
of the game with a hyper-intellectual mind and is a relatively skilled
orator. On the flip side, Brandel's also regarded by many players, fans,
and folks in the media as a know-it-all type who likes to stir the pot.
To say that he draws mixed reviews would be an understatement.

Six months before I joined Golf Channel, Brandel wrote a scathing critique of Tiger Woods following a season in which he won five
times. In the article, Chamblee handed out year-end grades for various
star players. Writing for Golf.com, he wildly gave Tiger an "F," arguing that he was essentially a cheater and shouldn't get any credit for
his wins because of four different rules infractions he'd committed.

In the piece, Brandel wrote, "I remember when we only talked about Tiger's golf. I miss those days. He won five times and contended in majors and won the Vardon Trophy and…how shall we say this… was a little cavalier with the rules." He later attempted to compare the aforementioned rules violations with him getting caught cheating on a test in fourth grade.

Soon after the op-ed, Tiger's agent, Mark Steinberg, put Brandel and Golf.com on notice. In a sharply worded statement to the media, Steinberg said, "There's nothing you can call a golfer worse than a cheater. This is the most deplorable thing I have ever seen, I'm not one for hyperbole, but this is absolutely disgusting. Calling him a cheater? I'll be shocked, stunned if something is not done about this. Something has to be done. There are certainly things that just don't go without response. It's atrocious. I'm not sure if there isn't legal action to be taken. I have to give some thought to legal action."

Soon after Steinberg's statement, Tiger addressed the Chamblee situation with Rory McIlroy during their one-on-one televised match in China. When asked by Rory about the controversy, Tiger responded: "…The ball really is in the court of the Golf Channel and what they are prepared to do." Wisely, even though Brandel's controversial op-ed was written for a *Sports Illustrated* entity, Tiger implied that Golf Channel needed to punish his antagonist for his indiscretion. Who could blame him? He was right to do so. After all, Chamblee received most of his notoriety and his money from the network, which gave him a voice in the first place.

Besides him and his agent, everyone from Tiger fans to other news organizations was on Brandel's case about his hit job piece. For instance, Bleacher Report's Richard Leivenberg wrote, "In an effort to raise his own profile, Chamblee has become strident and attacking, eschewing the basic principles of journalism. While singling out Tiger with his unfounded criticism and innuendo, Chamblee sounds like he is auditioning for an anchor position on Fox News." Finally, the following week Brandel somewhat apologized while talking live on-air with fellow Golf Channel host Rich Lerner. "I went too far," he admitted. "Cheating involves intent. There's no way that I could know with 100 percent certainty what Tiger's intent was in any of those situations. That was my mistake."

Obviously, there was no evidence that Tiger had made any type of rules infractions, so I was a bit bothered to read about my soon-to-be co-worker attacking his character in such an unfair and outspoken way. It was pretty clear that Brandel had some sort of bone to pick with Tiger back then for whatever reason.

Ironically, even after spending years promising viewers that Tiger was washed up, when Tiger had his comeback win in the 2019 Masters, suddenly Brandel began acting like he'd been pulling for him all along. By that point, though, the damage was done. To this day, I've never seen him walk a range at a PGA Tour event, but I can only imagine what the reaction might be.

———————

In the short period after I started working at Golf Channel, I rarely saw Brandel or interacted with him. The first time I remember attempting to engage with him happened one day when I saw him watching golf in what was known as the analyst room at the network. The small room had a couple of televisions mounted on the wall, and the analysts (and sometimes hosts and producers) would frequently hang out in there to watch the tournament action and prep for the show. Since I had a little time to spare that day and thought this would be a good opportunity to engage with our lead analyst, I walked in and sat down on a nearby sofa. We did this a lot at my previous job at the Big Ten Network. It helped create synergy between the hosts and analysts, which always made the shows better. Plus, it gives you a chance to get to know each other.

As soon as I sat down, I noticed that Brandel didn't acknowledge my presence. So I tried to break the ice by throwing him a softball about the tournament. He gave me a few curt, one-word answers while avoiding any eye contact. I tried again, this time about college football, since I knew he went to the University of Texas. Charlie Strong was in his first year as the Longhorns' head coach, so I asked his thoughts on the hire. His response couldn't have been colder. "I'm not a big football fan," he grumbled, returning to his notes. After an awkward minute or so, I took the hint, got up, and left.

My next real encounter with Brandel didn't happen until almost a year later. It was in October 2015, during a live breaking news broadcast. I was working *Golf Central* that night but was called in early because it'd just been announced that Tiger had undergone another back procedure. We went on-air early that day and kept going throughout most of the afternoon. I can tell you, it's mentally exhausting to be on live TV that long. Most of the interviews were call-ins because it was a breaking news story, and we didn't have anyone scheduled to come in. We interviewed players, former players, analysts, coaches, doctors—anyone we could get on the show to talk about it with us. Brandel was scheduled to be on *Golf Central* the following day but was flying in early from his home in Scottsdale to work the show that night because of the news about Tiger. As soon as he landed and got in his car, he was going to call in and do a phoner for the breaking news show. I only found this out a few minutes before the interview started. *Lucky me,* I thought. You don't prep for breaking news shows; they're done on the fly. It's like being in a race car that's going 185 mph.

As soon as he was patched through in the show, I began by asking him a simple question. I needed time while he answered that one to form the direction I wanted to go next since I just found out he was calling in. "Brandel, are you surprised by the news of Tiger having another procedure on his back?" While this isn't a cardinal sin in the broadcasting world, a general rule of thumb at Golf Channel was to avoid yes or no questions because the person you're interviewing could literally just answer with "yes" or "no" and leave you awkwardly hanging. Sure, I suppose an irked player could do that to you, but not a co-worker, right?

Wrong.

"Well," he sniffed before pausing for a snide-sounding laugh, "Yeah, I am." He let his answer trail off. Then...silence. Thrown for a loop, I paused, thinking he was going to say something else. Dead air. The abrupt lull felt like it went on for a minute, but I'm sure it was only a few painstaking seconds. Scrambling to not look foolish on camera, I followed his reply with a simple, "Okay, why?"

Before bothering to answer, he hemmed and hawed, again seeming to passive-aggressively imply to the viewers that I'd asked a dumb question. Doing my best to stay composed, I managed to get through the rest of his segment without showing any noticeable frustration.

When the show went to commercial, I was clearly annoyed. The analyst I was working with in studio and the floor director were surprised by his dismissiveness toward me. When I voiced my displeasure about what had happened afterward to Adam Hertzog, the director of news operations at the time, he said I should mention it to Brandel. I told him I was too annoyed to bring it up and not in the mood to have a blow-up with him. I'd heard stories of the many shouting matches he'd been involved in over the years.

The breaking news show ended not too long after, and within minutes of me discussing the interview with Adam, Brandel strolled into the newsroom. To my surprise (and frustration), Adam decided to announce for everyone to hear, "Hey, Brandel...Lisa isn't happy with how you gave her a one-word answer." He was kind of laughing when he said it, thinking it was funny, I suppose. Brandel immediately snapped back, "Well, maybe she should be more prepared next time then." I could feel steam starting to come out of my ears. I stood up and walked over to him. "How dare you question my preparedness in front of my co-workers, Brandel," I said sternly. "That's out of line. Don't you ever do that again." I went back to my desk, still fuming, while the room fell eerily silent. Meanwhile, Brandel marched out of the newsroom with a snide smirk on his face.

Surprisingly, the worst part of the encounter didn't even come from Brandel. About an hour or so later, Adam asked me into his office and demanded that I apologize to Brandel. He told me that Brandel said I'd embarrassed him in front of everyone, and because we had to work the show together that night, I had to apologize so it didn't make things uncomfortable on air. I couldn't believe it. I told Adam he'd lost his mind. This was Brandel's doing, and partly his, too, for bringing it up in front of everyone when I asked him not to. Then he told me if I didn't apologize, he'd send me home and have someone else host the show.

That son of a bitch, I thought. Both of them. I wish I'd just gone home. But instead, I walked into the green room and told Brandel that we needed to put this behind us and move on so we could work together. He barely said two words in response. Typical Chamblee.

Naively, I had no idea back then just how much power he held at the network and how this particular day would create a domino effect—one that would end up playing a significant role in my dismissal.

———————

Not long after I went public with my story about my treatment at Golf Channel, I started to learn more about Molly and Geoff's prized pundit. To this day, many golf fans probably still wonder why I've been so outspoken about Brandel being an analyst for some of the biggest events in women's golf. I've received comments from a lot of folks saying that just because I had an issue with him, it shouldn't prevent him from doing his job, no matter his gender. They defend him, saying things like, "He's earned the right to be in this position." In their defense, it's a logical position to take, considering I haven't divulged the story behind my strong opposition until now. Hopefully, the following will provide some clarity.

We all know that casual sexism exists everywhere. Often, the person who commits the violation doesn't even realize it's happened. That can easily be forgiven, especially if the person acknowledges the mistake and vows to be more mindful of it in the future. Unfortunately, society has ingrained this type of behavior into a lot of people. It doesn't make it right, but it does make it understandable. Then there's intentional sexism, which should never be tolerated, under any circumstance.

Toward the tail end of my time at Golf Channel, a female employee I worked with told me in detail about what she experienced one afternoon at work. She was in an office area and overheard Brandel and another male co-worker debating who had the best breasts on the LPGA Tour. They were laughing and joking about it, going back and forth with names. There was quite a bit of dialogue about this topic between them, which was taking place while coverage of an LPGA tournament was being broadcast on a TV where they were sitting. She purposely walked by to remind them she was there, but it didn't seem to matter. Their conversation continued without skipping a beat. Clearly, both men were unfazed by her presence.

She was appalled by their behavior. Of course, I'd never reveal the "winner" of their demeaning contest, but I can tell you that she still plays on tour. It's one of the many reasons I've been so adamantly opposed to Brandel working any tournament involving female players, especially LPGA players.

Not long after hearing that story, I also learned from a very credible source how Brandel had openly talked about life in America basically being better when women stayed home and raised their kids. Again, this happened while he was at an event representing Golf Channel. His words and actions certainly seem to suggest that he'd be perfectly happy if the clock was turned back to 1950.

CHAPTER 14

SARAH KEMP

THE FIRST TIME I met Sarah Kemp face-to-face was in January 2016 on a boat in the Bahamas. We were both there that week for the LPGA Tour's season-opener. Sarah's a professional golfer and was taking part in a photo shoot that afternoon, hitting golf balls from the top deck of an eye-catching vessel that was harbored nearby. Afterward, she was scheduled to do a sit-down interview with a couple of writers I know well. When they asked if I wanted to tag along, I immediately said yes. I've always been fascinated by yachts and private planes, knowing they're well out of my financial reach.

Part of my reporting assignments for Golf Channel included covering the LPGA five to seven times per season, which wasn't nearly enough given the amount the Tour pays the network to broadcast its tournaments. Golf Channel has never had, and still doesn't have, a full-time reporter for the LPGA Tour like it does the PGA Tour. This antiquated business decision could be a separate chapter in a different book. However, given the misogynist nature of the network, it shouldn't come as much of a surprise to anyone.

Similar to what happened with almost every player I'd met or interviewed over the years, anytime I ran into Sarah at a tournament from that point on, we'd say hi and have a quick chat. One of her closest tour mates (I use "mates" because Sarah's Australian) at the time was a player named Becky Morgan. In a roundabout sort of way, I got to know Becky through Sarah and discovered that she was regularly in Orlando because her coach lived there. Over time, I got to know them both very well but in entirely different ways.

By March 2017, what began as a casual friendship with Sarah had evolved into a relationship. While everything was great for me personally, I was starting to get concerned that this could pose a dilemma for me professionally. Before witnessing the swift and unfair elimination of Angela Akins (now Angela Garcia) because of her relationship with Sergio, I had no idea this sort of thing could be a fireable offense. I mean, you don't get to pick and choose who you fall in love with; it just happens. My situation, however, was much different than Angela's.

Unfortunately for Sarah, her 2016 season didn't go well, and she lost her full-time playing status on the LPGA Tour. Because of that, she was competing primarily on the Ladies European Tour, which I never covered, and Golf Channel hardly ever broadcast except for the end of the year when there wasn't a lot of other professional golf being played around the world to showcase.

Not long after we started seeing each other, I decided to disclose our relationship to Molly since Sarah and I knew she'd still occasionally play in an LPGA tournament because of the length of time she'd had full status in years past plus her final position on the prior season's money list. It took a couple of months to work up the courage, but I knew I couldn't put the conversation off any longer.

I remember vividly going into work that day like it was yesterday. I barely slept the night before. As soon as I sat down at my desk, I sent Molly's assistant an email and asked if I could talk to her for a few minutes. She scheduled me in for a small block of time early that afternoon. When I walked in, it was the usual Molly meet-and-greet—high-energy small talk for a minute or so and then down to business. I sat on her black leather sofa. She was behind her desk. I took a deep breath, and was nervously shaking as the words came out of my mouth: "I hope I'm not going to get fired for this…" She quickly interrupted with something like, "C'mon, Lisa. Don't be silly. What's going on?" I told her about Sarah, her not having full-time status anymore, my fear of how she'd react on the heels of the Angela situation—all of it.

This was the first time I'd ever seen a genuine human reaction from Molly. Her response was emphatic and to the point: "You're not getting fired, Lisa. Okay? I appreciate you telling me about it. If Angela had done the same, things probably would have worked out differently for her."

Feeling much lighter, I looked at Molly and said there was one more thing she needed to know. I'd finally worked up the courage to tell her now because Sarah was almost certain she would get into the field in the Northwest Arkansas Walmart Championship the following month, and I was scheduled to be on-site as a reporter. This was always one of my favorite weeks of the year because it's close to my hometown and a tournament that I've had strong ties to since its beginning.

Again, Molly couldn't have reacted any better. "Let me talk to Geoff about it and figure out how we want to proceed, but don't worry. One of us will be in touch soon. And, if it's okay, don't say anything to anyone about this just yet. We're still concerned that Angela may try to sue us, so I don't want to risk anything. Now, have a good show. We'll figure it out. And congratulations. I'm happy for you!"

Finally, I could breathe. I'd been dreading that conversation for a couple of months, and it went better than I'd imagined. I felt energized and relieved. A day or so later, on May 31, 2017, at 2:13 PM to be exact, I received the following text message from Molly:

"Geoff and I spoke about your personal issue. When u r back in, will u reach out to him? -M"

I replied, "Of course. Thanks."

I didn't think about it then because this was standard procedure in the Golf Channel news department. Geoff was involved in everything. But now that I'm away from it all, it's easy to see that this was, at best, unacceptable behavior. My boss was having me report to her husband, who didn't work in my department or oversee my job in any capacity (he was just the executive editor at this point), about my personal life. What if I wasn't comfortable talking with him about it but didn't have the courage to tell her because it's hard to say no to your boss, especially when it involves her husband?

Needless to say, as soon as that day came around, I just wanted it to be over. It was awkward walking into his office, with the door closing behind me, to talk about my relationship with Sarah and what it meant for my job moving forward. But I felt like I didn't have a choice. *Just get this over with,* I kept telling myself beforehand.

As uncomfortable as I felt initially, it did help that Geoff was quickly reassuring. He echoed the same sentiments as Molly a few days prior—my job was safe, and we could figure this out. He told me there were just a few things we needed to discuss. First, he and Molly had decided to take me off the Walmart tournament. He said they talked about it, and because of the potential legal action from Angela, they didn't want the appearance that it was okay for me to cover a tournament that Sarah was playing in while Angela wasn't given the same opportunity. He reiterated that this wasn't a punishment but more of them protecting themselves and the network. I told him I completely understood their decision, which I did at the time.

His second request was that if I attended a tournament Sarah was playing in during my time off not to wear any Golf Channel–logoed attire or use my Golf Channel–issued credential to access the grounds, clubhouse, etc. "Of course," I responded. These both seemed like very reasonable requests, and I assured him I'd follow those rules.

As I was leaving his office, Geoff asked what Sarah's name was so he could keep up with her scores. He said he'd be pulling for her privately, which I appreciated. Similar to my meeting with Molly, I felt much better walking out than I did walking in.

CHAPTER 15

OUTED

THE FIRST FEW MONTHS of my relationship with Sarah had its challenges, mainly because of me. Even though there were occasional difficulties with a very small group of overbearing co-workers, I still loved my job and was rattled by the possibility of losing it—much more than I ever let on. I'm sure those insecurities affected me both at home and at work. This was supposed to be a happy time, not one filled with so much internal turmoil. As most can attest, in the battle between happiness and worry, the latter seems to prevail almost every time. It certainly did with me.

The conversations with Molly and Geoff helped ease the concerns, because I felt like I now had a couple of powerful allies on my side. Life at work had settled down and was relatively calm between mid-June and mid-September of that year. As a result, things at home were getting much better, too. I was less stressed and more present with Sarah, which showed in how our relationship began to thrive.

Sarah and I are polar opposites in many ways but two peas in a pod in a lot of others. I'm your typical Virgo—outspoken, analytical, and a perfectionist. Meanwhile, Sarah is your typical Sagittarius—reserved with others and will do anything to avoid confrontation. While our personality traits may differ, we love life the same way. We're both very close to our families. Neither one of us has a large circle of friends. We're highly competitive. We love food way too much—planning the next meal before we're finished with the one we're currently consuming. (By the way, it's been a true blessing to have developed such a healthy relationship with food—while in the healthiest relationship of my life.) Best of all, in my opinion, we're both childishly silly. To this day, and probably forever, we joke about what people would think if they could see how goofy we are behind closed doors. They say there's someone for everyone in this world. Without a doubt, I found my *someone* in Sarah.

A big part of our connection early on centered around golf. Interestingly enough, we don't actually play together a lot these days because I don't play too much anymore. But I understand the game better than most because of my background and often go out with her on the course and act as an extra set of eyes for her and her coach, John Serhan, who lives in Australia. To be honest, I think John appreciates that more than she does. She just likes me being out there with her to take swing videos. Of course, I oblige to keep the peace.

Sarah had been playing golf all over the world that year, which isn't easy if you're on a tight budget. Life on the Ladies European Tour is much more difficult than on the LPGA, especially when you're based in the U.S. In early July 2017, she asked me if I wanted to caddie for her in Thailand, and after the tournament, we could take a vacation to Phuket—a well-known island on the western shore that's home to some of the country's most popular beaches. Best of all, Thailand is famously inexpensive, so, without hesitation, I said yes!

Despite the blistering heat, everything was going great that week so far. Sarah didn't win, but she made the cut and cashed a check, which is always nice for a player who's been struggling. After the tournament, we packed our bags and took the short flight to our next destination.

Phuket is beautiful and, like most of Thailand, very humbling to see in person. It is indeed a third world way of life. On our first full day there, Sarah had booked us on a journey to the famed James Bond Island—a protected landmark in Phang Nga Bay that's well known for its majestic charm and the role it played in the 1974 movie *The Man With the Golden Gun*. She said she'd wanted to go there for years. I showed my enthusiasm and then immediately Googled "James Bond Island."

The day couldn't have gone any better. It started with a 45-minute high-speed boat ride early in the morning to our stunning destination spot, where we played with monkeys, took a canoe ride under the magnificent limestone cliffs, and ate a chef-inspired lunch with 12 or so of our new friends. We also got to walk around the island, venture into dozens of small caves, and take photos.

This was my favorite photo we took that day, which I proudly posted on Facebook—something I rarely did—and tagged Sarah with these words:

Thailand... You're a beauty.
—with Sarah Kemp at James Bond Island.

It was the first time I'd shared a non-golf photo of the two of us on social media, and it would end up setting off alarm bells nearly 10,000 miles away in the Golf Channel newsroom in Orlando. I posted it that night in Phuket, 11 hours ahead of the Eastern Time Zone, right before going to sleep, and didn't think much of it.

When I woke up the next morning, my phone was full of notifications. I'd missed several calls from two co-workers, both of whom were good friends and knew all about Sarah and me, as well as my disclosure of our relationship to Molly and Geoff. There were text messages from both of them explaining why they were frantically calling. Something like, "Call us as soon as you wake up. You're not going to believe what's happened around here. It's a total shitshow. Everyone is talking about that photo."

What? I remember thinking to myself. This made no sense at all. I told Sarah the news and then immediately returned their calls. Within a few minutes, all three of us were on the phone. The way they explained it to me, someone had shown the photo I posted to Mark Summer (who didn't have a Facebook account) and pointed out that I was on vacation with an LPGA player. Whoever it was knew that Sarah was a player because, since I tagged her, it provided a direct link to her profile, which lists "Works at LPGA" as her job title, even though she'd lost her status on Tour. For the record, it also listed the same occupation for the Australian Ladies Professional Golf Tour and the Ladies European Tour, where she was primarily playing at the time.

My friends were ping-ponging back and forth their accounts of what had happened earlier that day. They explained that it was a total circus—something you'd expect to see in a soap opera, not at work. Mark was going up to young production assistants, asking to see their Facebook pages and pointing out "the photo." He was asking these people if they had any knowledge of my relationship with Sarah and if they were aware that she played on the LPGA Tour. He apparently kept going on and on about how he couldn't believe I'd do this knowing what had just happened to Angela. According to them, the entire conversation in the newsroom that day was barely about golf. Instead, it was about my personal life and the *professional sins* I'd just committed. These conversations weren't just among co-workers I knew well, either, but also between many I barely knew at all. I'd also later learn that within days of me posting that photo, there was a scheduling meeting in a conference room with 10 or so people in attendance. My Facebook profile was displayed on a computer screen during that meeting showing "the photo," which was discussed among the attendees. It felt like the worst kind of workplace backstabbing.

As I mentioned earlier, I've always been a private person, especially regarding my relationships. I'm sure part of that is because of my personality, and the other part results from spending all those years in the closet. I suppose some of the battles we fight personally never completely go away.

At the time, I'd only disclosed my relationship with Sarah to a handful of people at work, two of whom were Molly and Geoff. That's why this news, as much as it angered me for obvious reasons, didn't concern me too much. I knew my job was safe. Plus, Molly was the one who made the decision not to disclose my relationship to any of my other superiors because of the lingering possibility of Angela filing a lawsuit. I didn't ask her to do it.

I hadn't quite planned out how I wanted to handle my first day back at work after our Thailand trip. I thought I'd get in the office and discuss what I'd been told with Molly and Geoff before doing anything else. But I didn't get that chance. A few minutes after I walked in and got settled at my desk, Mark Summer and Adam

Hertzog came over and told me they wanted to meet with me in Geoff's office after the production meeting. While this was puzzling, I responded with a quick, "Okay," not knowing why they wanted to talk to me with Geoff in the room. Geoff knew about Sarah. *Why would he be involved in this conversation?* I wondered. The only thing I could think of was maybe they hadn't told him yet about what they *thought* they'd discovered.

Before revealing what happened next, let me just offer this one piece of advice to all women in the workplace: if three men in your office, one of whom is your boss' husband, insist that you participate in a closed-door meeting about a personal, romantic relationship, I implore you to please get up and walk out—or at the very least have someone on your side in the room with you. The mere fact that I was called into this meeting was, at first, extremely uncomfortable. But, upon reflection, it was also so wildly inappropriate that many people who know the story still can't believe it happened, especially me.

There were four sitting areas in Geoff's office. He was seated behind his desk. Mark and Adam were sitting in two chairs to his left, and I was on a sofa across from Geoff. Adam started the conversation.

"Lisa, we know you were on vacation with an LPGA player in Thailand, and we are also now aware that you told Molly and Geoff about your relationship with Sarah several months ago to protect yourself. But after learning about her, we looked into it, and you weren't honest with them about her playing status on the LPGA Tour."

The first thing I wanted to say back to him was, "You're a fucking idiot, Adam." But I remained calm for the time being and instead responded with, "So how did you come to this conclusion,

Adam?" I was already fuming inside but doing my best not to show it.

"Well," he began, "Sarah has played in 12 LPGA tournaments this year. That's not the schedule of someone who only has part-time status."

At this point, I couldn't help myself. I took a deep breath and said, "Adam, you work in golf, yet you have no idea what a player's status means? First of all, there's no such thing as part-time status. It's called conditional status." I was just getting warmed up. "Yes, Sarah's played in 12 LPGA events so far this season. She got into most of those because of her longevity on Tour, plus she played well in one of them early, which made her eligible for more later in the season. That's called having conditional status—meaning you're not a full-time player eligible to play a full schedule. She got into a couple of the other tournaments you're counting because they're co-sanctioned by the LET [Ladies European Tour], where she does have full status. You should probably get your facts straight before accusing me of something so egregious. Let's be honest here…you basically just called me a liar."

Then Mark jumped in, without even touching the *liar* comment, wanting to know why I told Molly and Geoff about Sarah but kept it from him and Adam. He said they deserved to be in the loop as well. I said I didn't tell him because he's the biggest gossip in the newsroom and just proved it once again. Also, that I didn't trust him after the way he reacted to Angela's situation, not to mention the time he publicly ridiculed a new analyst the year prior. We were in Eugene, Oregon, for the NCAA Golf Championships in May 2016. As the most senior person there that week, Mark was leading a work dinner one night with 20 or so people in attendance. At the beginning of the dinner, Mark made some remarks about the week ahead and then mocked a new analyst who, much to his embarrassment, had recently faced a small bout of anxiety while doing his first live report. We were all uncomfortable, and I was furious that he'd do such a thing, especially having faced my own bouts of anxiety on air in the past. Anyone who's experienced anxiety knows it's a horrible feeling and nothing to make fun of. As Mark continued, I stood up and said, "We don't do this, Mark. We don't talk about our co-workers like that. [He's] extremely bothered by what happened. It's nothing to laugh about." Mark said nothing in response and quickly sat down. In that memorable awkward moment, everyone got quiet.

Back to the meeting in Geoff's office. Still addressing Mark directly, I went on about how I'd received calls and texts from co-workers regarding his inappropriate behavior that day after being made aware of the photo I posted with Sarah. I also told him that I couldn't believe his unprofessional actions were, once again, on full display.

Geoff just sat there, not saying a word, and watched this ridiculous back-and-forth get even more heated. Finally, Adam dropped the bomb he'd been sitting on the whole time. He said they'd decided to remove me as the reporter from the only LPGA tournament I was scheduled to work the rest of the year—the CME Group Tour Championship. I was absolutely stunned and just shook my head in disbelief. Sarah wasn't even playing in the event, so it made no sense whatsoever. Until it did. That's when I realized they were removing me from it purely as punishment because they believed I'd lied about Sarah to Molly and Geoff.

By now, I'd had enough. I looked at Mark and Adam and said, "I need you both to leave. I need to talk to Geoff on my own." Adam tried to push back on leaving, but Geoff asked them to give us a couple of minutes. Once out the door, Geoff immediately said, "I'm sorry. I had no idea they were going to ambush you like that."

Had I been thinking clearly, I would've realized at that moment that Geoff wasn't the ally I thought he was. He had to have known about Mark and Adam removing me from the tournament; otherwise, he would've gotten involved in the discussion, knowing they were wrong with their assumption regarding Sarah's playing status on the LPGA Tour.

Instead, I treated him like he was innocently out of the loop, which was a big mistake on my part. Even with all the poor decisions Mark and Adam had made over the years at Golf Channel, there was still no way they would've removed me from a tournament over an issue involving my personal life unless it'd been approved somewhere up the chain of command (i.e., Molly and Geoff). Getting something like this wrong would've undoubtedly been an HR violation. Naively, I started talking to Geoff like he had no part in it, saying things like, "You've worked in golf for a long time. How do these two not know how a player's status on Tour works?"

The more I talked, the more Geoff must've realized that I was right. Twelve tournaments were just a little over one-third of the events on the schedule that season, and again, Sarah only played in two of those because of her status on the Ladies European Tour, not the LPGA Tour—which I'm sure he didn't connect the dots on before. When I finished, he said, "Let me talk to Molly about getting you back on CME. I don't think taking you off it is right."

When I walked out of his office, I was so furious I was shaking, and it was about to get even worse. Within a few minutes, Chantel McCabe (another reporter) and Chris Datres (a field producer assigned to work CME) told me they already knew I'd been taken off the tournament and that Chantel was my replacement. Then, after talking with others about it, I realized that almost everyone in the newsroom knew about my removal before I did. Once again, typical behavior at Golf Channel.

The following week Molly asked me to have breakfast with her away from the office so we could discuss what had happened. The breakfast went as well as could be expected. I told her precisely what took place in the meeting with Mark and Adam and explained why their accusations were not only incorrect but also terribly unfair. I'd been upfront with Molly and Geoff about an issue that I wasn't comfortable discussing with my bosses. But I did it because I felt I had to, based on what happened with Angela the year prior, and I didn't want to do anything to jeopardize my job.

When our breakfast ended, she told me she would talk to Mark. She thought I needed to be back on the schedule to work the tournament. One week later, on October 9, 2017, at 1:53 PM, I received the following text message from Molly: "You are covering CME. Let's chat again later this fall once you know your girlfriends commitment to LPGA next year. Best, M"

I never thought to ask her why it took so long to give me this answer. As the executive producer, the buck stops with Molly when it comes to on-air assignments. Now I wonder how many people were actually involved in the decision. How high up the chain of command did this go? It still amazes me that no one apologized for what occurred—not Molly, Geoff, Mark, or Adam. They just put me back on the tournament schedule and hoped the problem would quickly fade away.

As you can imagine, even though I'd been reinstated, everything about my job was different from that point on. All of this had *severely* damaged the honor (and adoration) of working at Golf Channel. Yes, I was angry. But I was also deeply hurt by it, too.

Mark was my day-to-day boss, and our relationship would never be the same again.

To this day, I wonder how long it took him to start orchestrating his carefully calculated comeback. I have to hand it to him...he'd end up hitting me much harder the next time around.

CHAPTER 16

UNSCATHED

IT'S COMPLICATED TO think about what I call "the Thailand incident." Initially, I felt validated by winning the battle and getting put back on the tournament schedule. I was right. Mark and Adam were wrong. End of story. But that's not how it works when people have an agenda, and I should've known better.

In all of my public outcries and accusations against Golf Channel since my contract ended, this is the one story I haven't breathed a word of publicly until now—mainly because it involves my personal life. Most people who follow me on social media can easily interpret that I'm in a relationship with Sarah even though I've never used the word *partner*—or now *wife*, since we got married on December 15, 2020—to describe her. I realize that I'm almost too private with that part of my life. Hopefully, by revealing more of myself in this book, I'll finally let go of most of those insecurities once and for all.

But that's not the point. The point is what anyone chooses to reveal about her or himself should always be that person's decision. Of all the violations Golf Channel committed during my employment, every lawyer—including my own—always says this one was the most illicit of them all.

Initially, I didn't feel demeaned by their actions. I was furious. Regardless, by going around the office, showing people our vacation photo, and trying to dig up dirt on me, Mark Summer essentially outed me at work, which is a clear violation of any employee's con-stitutionally protected rights.

I hadn't been forthcoming with details about my personal life with most of my co-workers for various reasons, but that was my choice to make, not Mark's. The fact that neither Molly nor Geoff acknowledged how wrong this was, never held him accountable, and never even apologized to me was reprehensible. When Mark and Adam told me I wasn't going to work the CME tournament, it wasn't just humiliating—it felt like an attack on my relationship with Sarah and, even more so, my character.

I'll go back to my HR friend mentioned earlier in the book. This is how she responded to the situation: "The moment that [Mark] outed you to all the other people at work, it was an invasion of your privacy and harassment. It was a huge event in the office, and you weren't even there to take care of it or defend yourself. It led to a wildfire of allegations that you had to put out on your own. The aftermath of it all was handled so poorly by them. It can be filed not just under harassment, but also sexual harassment and defamation of character."

She went on to reiterate, "Under the definition of harassment, Mark's intentions did not have to necessarily be bad for his behavior to still qualify as harassment." Typically, in a situation like the one Mark dragged me into, she offered this as the most likely outcome had it been handled properly: "The offending employee would at mini-mum be moved to a different department or transferred out of the general work area that we shared. At worst, Mark could have been fired for misdeeds that were so egregious, and the fact he walked away unscathed is nearly unheard of."

What's still surprising is how confident they seemed to be that I wouldn't take the matter any further. According to my lawyer, the way they consistently bungled these situations was one of our greatest strengths with the EEOC charges we filed. We wanted it legally documented that Golf Channel's top brass wasn't just aware of but complicitly involved in the active invasion of my privacy and defamation of my name. Any claim of ignorance on their part is unacceptable and easily disprovable.

Another friend of mine, who's been active in the human rights movement for almost 40 years, offered her thoughts on why honoring someone's privacy, especially regarding their sexual orientation, is so important.

"The issue of protecting one's right to sexual identity privacy in the workplace cannot be understated. It is a major issue facing people of various sexual orientations, and one that still doesn't get enough attention, especially from male, heterosexual managers."

There have been numerous examples of these privacy laws being upheld in federal courts. In November 2000, a Philadelphia Appeals Court ruled that demanding to know someone's sexual orientation through forced disclosure was unconstitutional. The judges released a statement after the decision, famously stating, "[I]t is difficult to imagine a more private matter than one's sexuality…"

From that day forward, my private life no longer seemed to be completely private at Golf Channel. I can only imagine how much this was discussed when I wasn't around—in the newsroom, down the halls, upstairs in the dining area, etc. I have no doubt it spread outside the network, too. People seem to love juicy stories like this, especially in the media. Even though I never spoke a word about it with anyone at work outside my small circle of friends, everyone knew what had happened. The damage was done, and there was no going back.

CHAPTER 17

HUSBAND AND WIFE

WHEN I STARTED my job at Golf Channel, I don't recall being aware that Molly's husband also had a high-ranking position at the network. It seemed a bit strange when I first found out but it wasn't something I put too much thought into since I assumed, as the executive editor, I wouldn't be working with him very often.

According to his bio on the network's website, "Prior to joining Golf Channel in March 2012, [Geoff] Russell held the post of editor-in-chief for *Golf World* magazine, a Conde Nast publication and sister magazine to *Golf Digest*." From what I've been told, Molly and Geoff were a package deal. She wouldn't take the job unless her husband was offered a role with the company, too.

In 2017, just weeks after the "Thailand incident," Molly and the powers that be at the network thought it'd be a good idea to put her husband in charge of the newsroom to oversee the on-air talent, despite having no experience whatsoever in production. This meant they'd basically be working in tandem—even though he didn't report directly to his wife, but instead to the president of Golf Channel. At the same time as Geoff's "realignment" (as they called it), Molly was promoted from a senior vice president to an executive vice president (with a nice raise, I'm sure). It was a bizarre situation that no one I knew in the building could wrap their heads around—corporate nepotism at its finest.

I remember meeting Geoff at the office a week or two after my employment began. Much like with Molly, my first impression of him was positive enough, although I do recall thinking that he seemed to be more serious and straightforward than his wife. We didn't interact too often initially, but I noticed how he appeared to keep a watchful eye over the newsroom.

The first time I stepped foot in Geoff's office, I noticed a large dry-erase board on the wall behind his desk with many of the names of the on-air talent written on it in red, including mine. I wondered why the head of the editorial department had all of our names on his office wall. I assumed it was because part of the editorial department had to do with online and digital content, and some of those areas included the on-air talent. But after his promotion to an unqualified position, I couldn't help but think that perhaps they'd been preparing for his upward mobility long before any of us realized.

―――――――

According to Florida state law, where Golf Channel was based at the time, "Nepotism is the act of favoring someone for employment purposes, such as hiring or promoting, due to a non-work relation-ship, such as friendship, romantic relationship, or familial connec-tion." Under Florida law, public officials are banned from "appointing, promoting, employing, advancing, or advocating for an appointment, employment, promotion, or advancement in or to a position in the agency in which he serves or over which he exercises jurisdiction or control any individual who is a relative."

While these state laws specifically apply to publicly held govern-ment positions, most corporations like Golf Channel/NBCUniversal have nearly identical employee policies. There are corporate policies addressing anti-nepotism regulations in all 50 U.S. states. Most busi-nesses know it's essential to safeguard their organizations against any number of pitfalls that can accompany family members having too much absolute power between themselves. Somehow, when Molly lobbied for Geoff to be hired when she came on board, NBCUniver-sal didn't care enough about a potential power imbalance to nix the alleged demand.

When I asked my friend in HR to reflect on Molly and Geoff being the first and second chain of command for on-air talent, she was shocked that Golf Channel/NBCUniversal was okay with it.

"Nepotism can create problems with supervision, security, safety, and morale," she began. "As far as supervision goes, married partners in their positions create a fear of both managers and a perceived lack of impartiality. When addressing security, the supervisors may betray confidentiality, and this potential problem can lead to a subordinate's sense of tentative job security. Also, when you have family at play in the office space, there are more potential emotional triggers and/or conflict between the family members."

When I asked her if she'd ever experienced the effects of nepotism while she was working in corporate America, she relayed this story:

"I worked at a company where my boss was secretly married to the head of the department, making him the third-ranked employee down from the president. My boss' son threatened people in the office, saying that if they didn't do what he said, he would leverage that relationship by having his mom fire them. This created a sense of fear, distrust, and low morale."

Nepotism creates problems because it can influence decision-making in areas where family members are reporting to each other. Family members bring complex emotional relationships with all the baggage that it carries, and it's often hard to separate business from personal decisions. Also, nepotistic management lends itself to crony-ism by tacitly allowing friends of the family members luxuries and concessions that mere acquaintances in the company don't get.

As I continued working under Molly and Geoff, it was apparent there were certain "untouchable" employees who just so happened to be a part of their inner circle of friends. Though they never stated this out loud, the rest of my co-workers and I knew who these untouch-ables were and we knew that if we took issue with any of them, we'd likely get saddled with blame for their behaviors. This made conflict resolution extremely tricky when their buddies were doing things at work they shouldn't have been doing. It also emboldened those people to treat the rest of us however they saw fit.

Another quote from my friend in HR stood out when viewing nepotism purely from a gender perspective: "Men are hired for their potential while women are hired for what they've done."

As any professional woman can attest, we've historically hard to work harder than our male contemporaries to get ahead in business. Add to it the cronyism and nepotism that's already been addressed, and it makes it nearly impossible for women (and less-well-connected men) to get what they rightly deserve.

Upon further consideration of the potential versus accomplish-ments issue, I know how hard it is to be objective when considering my close friends and family for anything of importance. Moreover, if the issue involves work-related feedback, it requires extreme levels of diplomacy with these folks to keep things from going off the rails emotionally.

For most people, criticism isn't easy to accept. But when it's com-ing from individuals whose most significant flaws we're already aware of, it's even harder to accomplish the desired result: fixing whatever needs to be fixed.

When we love and care about someone, we want to see them succeed. It tempts us to make too much of their successes and to easily excuse their mistakes. To me, this combination of factors is the biggest reason why nepotism is so insidious in the workplace. After Geoff was promoted to No. 2 in the Golf Channel production hierarchy, he quickly proved to me how underqualified he was for his new managerial position.

Soon after Geoff replaced Adam Hertzog, he called me into his office to let me know they were extending my contract to a sixth year. This was standard operating procedure for on-air talent at the network—we were given two-year guaranteed contracts with an option for a third year, and this was my second time going through the extension process. The first thing that was odd about the meeting was that it happened much earlier than when they'd usually announced our extensions in the past. It was in the spring when Geoff informed me of this news, about eight months before my (second) two-year contract expired. Typically, three months or so was the norm. Still, I was happy they were extending me again and didn't think much about it. I loved the job and wanted nothing more than to keep learning and growing in my role.

But that wasn't what was eyebrow-raising in my meeting with Geoff. When I sat down, he led off with, "I just wanted to let you know that we've decided to pick up the option on your third year. We're very pleased with your performance. It's the first time I've done this, and I don't really know all that's involved in terms of feedback with your job. I'm not a TV person, but maybe you can get with Mark [Summer] and see what his thoughts are."

Here was the man who was now my boss and the head of the news operation telling me that he didn't know how to give me feedback because he didn't come from a production background. Again, although I was excited they were re-upping me for another year, my new boss (and Molly's husband) had just admitted to me that he essentially wasn't qualified for his job.

There was plenty of scuttlebutt around the office about Geoff's perceived ineptitude after he got promoted. The biggest thing that everyone noticed once he got elevated to his new role was how we started seeing less and less of him by the day. A common joke in the newsroom was, "Now that Geoff has this promotion and a big raise, all he does is come in for a few hours a day and then leaves to go play golf."

It was such a weird dynamic between Geoff and the rest of us. From the beginning, everyone (including many people who still work there) would talk about his inexperience and constant absence behind his back and then suck up to him when he was around. No matter what we thought of him, he was our new boss, and it was in all of our best interests to stay on his good side, especially considering who his wife was.

CHAPTER 18

THE FINAL STRAW

LIVE TELEVISION WAS a nervy test at times, but my heart was pumping this night. Seated to my immediate at times left was the rival I never wanted: Brandel Chamblee. I was filling in for a fellow host who needed the night off and called me at the last minute to take his place. It was always tougher working with Brandel, not just because I knew he despised me, but because it was usually during the most viewed time slots of *Golf Central*. I could feel the extra eyeballs watching me, especially his.

The show had been moving along rapidly, nothing out of the ordinary. Suddenly, as I was talking, a graphic that I didn't recognize with several different stats appeared on the screen, and I was having a hard time making sense of it. I'm not sure how I'd missed it in my pre-show preparation, but there it was. I could feel my pulse rapidly picking up speed. *This isn't good,* I thought to myself. Even with the pressure rising, this wasn't my first rodeo either. So I hung in there, doing my best to keep talking confidently and getting back on track. Meanwhile, I could see Brandel going ballistic out of the corner of my eye.

Arms flailing wildly in the air, unseen by the cameras, he had a full-fledged conniption fit. It was as if I'd just insulted his wife or mother on-air. Instead of doing what any other analyst or co-host would do in this situation and try to help save me from my mistake, he was doing everything in his power to make it worse.

Unequivocally, it was the worst experience I've ever had with another person on live TV in all my years in broadcasting. The moment the show ended, I was out the door. Even though I wanted to confront him about it, I knew that would only play into his hand. This is a man who thrives on controversy. If I snapped on the crown prince, it was straight to the guillotine. So, I just got the hell out of there instead.

The moment I got home, I called and unloaded to Geoff. At that point, I still thought he was an ally. Even though I was irritated about what had just happened, I made it clear to Geoff from the beginning of our conversation that my intent wasn't to bust Brandel or punish him. I just wanted some sort of resolution to this ridiculous ongoing feud we still had. Geoff told me he'd talk to Brandel and the producers and do his best to help. I thanked him for the time and told him I was tired of the thorny relationship with Chamblee and needed his assistance to smooth things over. The war between us had gone on for way too long. We needed a mediator with some clout to intervene, and Geoff seemed like the best person to do it.

Unfortunately, Geoff and I never discussed what took place that night until four months later, during a scheduling meeting about another assignment. That's when, out of the blue, he brought up that night in August on air with Brandel. Geoff was angry and immediately turned the conversation to that incident. Pointing his finger directly at me, he said, "It's always something with you. I asked Brandel and the producers about what happened, and they all came up with the same conclusion. It was just another mistake you made."

How was I supposed to respond to that? Of course I've made mistakes on air. I didn't need him to tell me that. And when I did make a one, I spent plenty of time beating myself up for it. No one's harder on me than I am. Besides, I never said the error that night with the graphic wasn't my mistake. But regardless of whose *fault* it was, it didn't warrant the over-the-top outburst from Brandel, especially during a live show. No one makes mistakes on purpose, so why react that way?

The problem now was that I'd once again somehow challenged their golden boy and appeared to be paying the price for it. It was the only thing that made sense. I had co-workers who warned me this would happen. Though there are numerous examples of Brandel's malignant narcissism, the most significant death blow to his credibility was when I learned that he was lobbying Molly to fire me...and had been for a while.

CHAPTER 19

THE BEGINNING OF THE END

DECEMBER 10, 2018: the day I received an email revealing my long-term fate with Golf Channel. This email didn't contain words to me personally. It was a scheduling email listing all of the on-air assignments for the first six months of 2019. This was the day I knew, without question, that my time with the network was coming to an end.

Before detailing that story, it's essential to go back to my first year working at Golf Channel to fully explain the situation. On September 28, 2014, I got the following email from a man named Mike McGee. Mike is the husband of Annika Sorenstam—the person who most would agree is the greatest female golfer of all time.

> Lisa,
>
> Thank you again for your help tonight. You were super. It was a very special evening and the start of something great. We appreciate you being there.

I'll get you some better pics than these. :-)

Best,

Mike

That night I'd emceed a ceremony announcing the first recipient of the Annika Award, which is now given annually to the Most Outstanding Female Collegiate Golfer of the Year. Molly was copied on the email Mike sent, and she responded to me the next morning at 7:17:

Thanks for doing this. Really important to keep getting you out there as a face of golf channel and women's college golf.

This was an important time for Golf Channel. The network had signed a deal with the NCAA to broadcast its women's and men's national championships in back-to-back weeks for the first time ever beginning the following year. There was a great deal of publicity and excitement surrounding the news. *Golf Central* would have a robust presence—a full studio set onsite to showcase the events and present our news shows live from the host course. The goal was for it to have the same look and feel as our major championship coverage, and I was going to be a part of this big stage for the first time in my career. Having been pegged by Molly to, as she worded it, be "a face of golf channel and women's college golf" was a significant moment for me personally, too.

Given my background as a collegiate golfer, she told me I was the perfect person to host the women's event onsite every year. This was a role that I not only took great pride in but always had circled on my calendar. I was also honored to continue hosting the Annika Award presentations every fall and to get to know Annika and Mike on a personal level as a result.

Fast-forward to late 2017. I received a couple of calls from two individuals with close ties to the University of Arkansas—one was a member of the athletics department, and the other was a considerable donor to the athletics department. Their messages were the same. The University was going to make a strong pitch to host the NCAA Division I Women's and Men's Golf Championships in 2019, and they wanted to know if I'd be willing to write a letter to the organization on the school's behalf.

Of course, I was thrilled with this news and agreed to do it immediately. As the first scholarship player in program history in the post–Title IX era for the University of Arkansas women's golf team, it'd be a dream come true to host a nationally broadcast event in my hometown. The following year, that dream was about to become a reality when the NCAA selected Arkansas to stage its 2019 championships.

So back to that dreadful day in December 2018 when I received the scheduling email. If you'll recall from the last chapter, this was four months removed from Brandel's outburst on air because of a mistake I made during the show, which resulted in my calling Geoff Russell for help.

I opened the email and saw the schedule attached at the bottom, so I clicked on the attachment to bring it up full screen. I had my brand-new 2019 calendar out and was ready to start marking down dates—in the studio versus reporting, using a different highlighter to color code the weeks at home versus on the road. I'm still old-fashioned in that sense, using a notebook-style calendar instead of an online version. I was going month-by-month, writing and highlighting away, as I did every time our schedule was released. January. February. March. April. May…

Wait, hang on. There's a mistake here, I thought. I was listed as a reporter for the women's NCAA championships, which comprise both the team and individual national titles—even though I'd never reported for either of these events before. Not to mention, the reporter's role is much less prominent than hosting, especially when it's onsite with a profound studio presence.

I immediately called Mark Summer since he was directly involved in scheduling the on-air talent. This wasn't a mistake, he informed me. They'd decided to have me report this year, and George Savaricas would host both the women's and men's championships. I couldn't quite wrap my head around what he'd just said, so I got dressed and went into work even though I was off that day. In fact, I wasn't working the rest of the year. This was the downtime for many of us since there wasn't much competitive golf being played anywhere around the world.

I walked into the building to get some answers. The first person I saw was Chantel, who immediately asked me what I was doing there on my day off. She could tell something was wrong. When I told her what I'd just learned from the scheduling email about our assignments for the NCAAs, she (once again) couldn't believe I was just now finding out. She said that Mark had shared the news with her weeks earlier that I'd be reporting for the women's event next year, and she'd have the same duties the following week for the men. Since Chantel began working at the network in 2017, she'd always reported for both the women's and men's NCAA championships. None of this made sense to either of us.

On a mission, I went directly into Mark's office. Of all the reprehensible things he'd done to me over the years, this felt like the most flagrant of them all because of the sentimental value it represented. When I walked in, he was sitting behind his desk with a smug grin on his face while I demanded some answers. The only response he gave me about why George was hosting instead of me was: "We just think he's better than you."

He let that line hang in the air, stinging like the slap in the face it was undoubtedly meant to be. My mind was reeling from the blow. *Better than me.* What did that even mean? "In what way?" I asked. He just shrugged his shoulders.

No one had ever told me there was any issue with my hosting during the NCAA championships all those years. The only feedback I received was overwhelmingly positive inside and outside the building, and my year-end reviews solidified that feedback. There was zero indication this would ever happen, especially at a place so dear to my heart. But looking back, I realize that's why they did it. It was cold and calculated and with a purpose.

I stormed out of Mark's office and walked next door to Geoff's. I thought maybe he could help sort out this mess. Certainly, he didn't know about the demotion, I naively assumed. At this point, I still foolishly thought he was an ally.

Geoff must've heard my outburst with Mark because he was waiting for me, just sitting there in anticipation of the moment. As soon as I walked in, with Mark following behind, he stood up and exploded into a fit of rage. He loudly announced that I shouldn't expect to cover the NCAAs just because they were in my hometown. "That's not how it works," he said. Then the real "a-ha moment" came next when he pivoted off that topic and began laying into me for my part in the August flare-up with Brandel, which completely threw me for a loop.

This was the first time we'd spoken about that night since I called Geoff after it happened. He blamed me for Brandel's reaction, saying he only did it because he cares about the shows and hates mistakes.

What stood out most while all of this was going on was the twisted enjoyment he and Mark seemed to have watching me suffer. Suddenly, I could read the writing on the wall. My feud with Brandel and my rocky history with Mark had led to this moment. Mark got his payback from the prior year's CME embarrassment when he had to put me back on the schedule, and Geoff was protecting the network's lead analyst, who could apparently do no harm.

I would've bet money that Geoff and Brandel had been waiting for this very moment since the August meltdown. Mark's wait had been even longer. But now, he had some powerful accomplices in his corner. My humiliating demotion was nothing more than retaliation for standing up to Chamblee with a side helping of old-fashioned trigger bait. All three men knew I'd be devastated by this news, and they were right. Their mission was accomplished. Any adverse emotion I displayed would be painted as my false sense of entitlement, inflated ego, and bitterness of being passed over for the high-profile position.

I knew that day my job with Golf Channel was on its last leg. As soon as I left, I called my dad and told him everything. He took a deep breath and responded very matter-of-factly, as he always does: "I hate to tell you this, Lisa, but I think you should start looking for another job."

PART IV

SHOTS FIRED

———

CHAPTER 20

BEWARE: HR

―――――――

I **WALKED OUT OF** Geoff's office that day knowing I had to do something. But I also knew there was no way in hell I was going to get Golf Channel's HR department involved. Not a chance. I'd heard—and witnessed—way too many sinister stories over the years. Most of those stories involved the network's head of human resources, Julie Lusk, and how she often enabled retaliation and treated those who reported complaints as if they were the ones on trial. There was a general sentiment around Golf Channel that Julie and the HR department, like Molly and Geoff, simply didn't care about major malfunctioning issues involving management and the network's stars.

From my perspective, the Angela/Sergio fiasco was awful enough, but an incident that occurred the following year was even worse. That summer, a young woman in her late twenties was viciously antagonized by an established veteran employee in his mid-fifties over an issue that was entirely out of her control. When something happened he disapproved of involving a story that was scheduled to air that week, he initiated several caustic, profanity-laced conversations with her—via phone calls and voicemail—one of which included telling her that "Any trained monkey could do your job!"

Just think about that for a minut*e. Any trained monkey could do your job.* Such a recklessly insensitive and demeaning statement after repeatedly screaming every profane word he could at her. I know how out of line he was because the woman he did it to played me a voicemail of one of his rants. Knowing something that terrible was a punishable offense, not to mention potential grounds for dismissal, we were both shocked when Molly, Julie, and the HR department did almost nothing to this man whatsoever. To make it even worse, Molly was the person spearheading the "let's just pretend it didn't happen" campaign. She wasn't even going to make him apologize at first, which is something I'll never understand.

When this young woman—and several other people, including her direct boss and me—came forward again, emphasizing that something had to be done about it, they finally made him *sort of* apologize. I say sort of because he didn't even look her in the eye when he got in touch. He called her back reluctantly a couple of days later and dodged all the traditional apologetic language, instead dancing around the issue: "Come on…you know we're good. I've never thought of you like that. You know I didn't mean it."

Not only did his half-assed mea culpa suffice to those in authority, but there was barely any punishment for him at all—and it wasn't the first time he'd unleashed this type of behavior on a female co-worker. By comparison, when I reported facts about Mizuno and refused to take a similar tongue-lashing from Geoff Russell, I was the person who was sent home from the tournament for reasons that, to this day, still haven't been properly explained. Meanwhile, this man, who called a female co-worker less than a "trained monkey," went back to work the same night he committed these terrible transgressions with only the softest slap on the wrist.

At home with my sister, Tracy
(Fayetteville, Arkansas—1977)

With my golf mentor, Jerry Hart (1992)

In the Lincoln Bedroom at the White House (1996)

With Hillary at a campaign event (Cincinnati, Ohio—2007)

Seeing Tiger Woods for the first time since our junior golf days (The Alotian Club, Roland, Arkansas—2006)

Caddying for John Daly in a practice round of the 2014 PGA Championship at Valhalla Golf Club (Louisville, Kentucky)

With my parents and Tracy at my induction into the Fayetteville High School Hall of Greats Ceremony (Fayetteville, Arkansas—2016)

At my parents' 50th wedding anniversary celebration—from left: my nephew, Bo; me; Dad; Mom; Tracy; my niece, Olivia (Fayetteville, Arkansas—2016)

Sharing stories with Justin Timberlake and Bill at the American Century Championship (Lake Tahoe, Nevada—2017)

With my parents at the Walmart NWA Championship (Rogers, Arkansas—2017)

With Sarah at a jazz bar (Chicago, Illinois—2017)

On set with Tripp Isenhour and Tim Rosaforte at Bay Hill (Orlando, Florida—2018)

Interviewing Steph Curry at the American Century Championship (Lake Tahoe, Nevada—2018)

Interviewing Rory McIlroy at the WGC Bridgestone Invitational at Firestone CC (Akron, Ohio—2018)

With James Patterson, Sarah, Bill, and Susan Patterson (Orlando, Florida—2018)

With the crew in Studio A (Golf Channel Studios/Orlando—2018)

With Bill (Naples, Florida—2018)

With Sarah and my cousins—from left: Carrie, Allison, and Rush—at the American Century Championship (Lake Tahoe, Nevada—2019)

With my family at my induction into the Arkansas State Golf Association Hall of Fame (Little Rock, Arkansas—2019; photo courtesy of ASGA)

Hosting my final *Golf Central* (with Tripp Isenhour and Tim Rosaforte—November 13, 2019)

Interviewing Lexi Thompson at the CME Group Tour Championship (Naples, Florida—2019)

Sharing a laugh with Tiger at the Hero World Challenge (Albany, Bahamas—2019; photo courtesy of Sunshine Photographics)

With Sarah and Bill (Orlando, Florida—2022)

Caddying for Sarah in the Evian Championship (Évian-les-Bains, France—2022)

With all of this in mind, I decided to try and find someone at NBCUniversal to talk to who could help ease my concerns and hopefully make me feel safe—especially considering my contract was coming up for renewal later that year. Completely lost about where to turn, I went to NBC.com to find some answers. Once there, I discovered NBCUniversal's Compliance Department and did a quick Google search on the role that compliance departments serve for companies like NBCUniversal. The word *compliance* alone piqued my interest. Immediately, I found something that stood out and made me want to get in touch with someone in that department: "A compliance officer is an employee of a company that ensures the firm is in compliance with its outside regulatory and legal requirements as well as internal policies and bylaws." That was enough for me. It wasn't the HR department and, by definition, was supposed to care about internal policies. Surely, someone in this office could give me some proper guidance.

I quickly discovered that NBCUniversal's Head of Compliance was a woman named Susanna Zwerling, so I made the call. After several rings, her voicemail picked up, and I left her a message asking her to call me—not revealing too much other than my name, my job title at Golf Channel, and that I needed to speak with her as soon as possible.

To her credit, Susanna got back to me later that day. At the beginning of our conversation, I made it clear why I was reaching out to her rather than Golf Channel's HR department, and I wanted her assurance that none of what I was about to tell her would get back to them out of fear of retaliation. She agreed without hesitation.

Susanna listened intently as I divulged my entire story—everything that had happened since I started working at the network, from my initial encounter with Mark Summer in Eugene, Oregon, to his later outing me at work and trying to pull me off the CME event. I recounted all the episodes with Brandel Chamblee leading up to my demotion at the NCAA tournament. At one point, the "any trained monkey" incident came up, and I explained why it made me not want to talk with Golf Channel's HR department as a direct result of its outcome. Most importantly, I made it very clear that I wanted all of my statements documented because I was worried that these very same people were trying to get me fired.

Susanna assured me that she took my claims seriously and needed a little time to follow up on everything. She told me she wanted to talk it over with some people in the legal department whom she trusted and asked if it'd be alright to share my name. Naively, knowing that Susanna was a lawyer made me feel safe enough to say okay. Since it was the holiday season, she asked if I could give her a couple weeks and said that if I hadn't heard from her by the new year to give her a call. As nervous as I was playing all my cards with a complete stranger, I left that conversation feeling hopeful that someone would finally take my problems seriously.

When January 2 rolled around, and I still hadn't heard back from Susanna, I called and left her a voicemail saying that I was just checking in to see if there was any update. The following afternoon, I was on the golf course with Sarah in Naples, Florida, and noticed that I had a missed call from a New York number. Seconds later, a voicemail notification appeared. What I heard in that message made my heart pound: "Lisa, Hi, it's Susanna Zwerling. Thanks for your message. Wanted to check in with you and let you know that Julie Lusk will follow up with you, but please send me an email or give me a call if that's a concern for you, and I'll have somebody else follow up." Freaking out, I called her back immediately and she answered. "Susanna, I only called you because I didn't want Golf Channel HR to be involved. I made that very clear from the start of our first conversation." After an awkward moment of silence, she said, "Okay, I'm going to have someone else take this over then. Let me put you in touch with Kaitlin Kertsman from Comcast Sports Philadelphia."

As you can imagine, I was beyond rattled by that call with Susanna. How could she have ignored my initial request after repeatedly telling her about my feelings toward Golf Channel's HR department? I now regretted *ever* making that call to her in the first place. I kept telling myself what an idiot I was for being so unsuspecting.

The next day, I received a call from Kaitlin, who couldn't have been more willing to help. I could tell that she genuinely cared about the situation and wanted to ensure someone was looking out for me. But even as great as Kaitlin was, she could only serve as a mediator at this point. When we first spoke, I told her that my biggest concern was knowing Susanna had let the cat out of the bag to Julie and Golf Channel after I'd explicitly told her not to. I needed Kaitlin to find out who at the network knew about this and, most importantly, that if Molly Solomon did, I was doomed. I told her that my job was over if Molly knew that I went to NBCUniversal or HR about all of this. Kaitlin assured me, "No, Lisa, that's not how it works. Let me find out what's up, and I'll call you back."

I'll never forget when she delivered the news: January 25, 2019. I was covering the Farmers Insurance Open in La Jolla, California. Kaitlin called while I was standing just off the 18th green, preparing for a post-round interview with Rory McIlroy. He was finishing up his second to last hole of the day and would soon be headed my way. When I answered, she cut right to the chase.

"Lisa...I'm so sorry to tell you this, but, yes, Molly knows about it. I talked to Julie Lusk, and she said there's nothing to worry about but that Molly has been informed about what's happened."

My internal reaction: *Fuck me.*

"You should have been told this upfront," Kaitlin continued, "but any time someone wants to have something that happened at work documented, we have to investigate."

"It would've been nice if Susanna had told me that on the front end because I never would've said anything to her," I responded.

Kaitlin stayed on the phone while I nervously reiterated that my job was over now that Molly knew about what had happened. Again, she tried to reassure me that it wasn't that bad. "Not to worry," she said to me. I told Kaitlin, "You don't know Molly. That's not how she operates." Kaitlin promised to talk with Julie and see if she could arrange a meeting between the two of us to try and calm my fears. I agreed even though I knew it wouldn't help. The damage had already been done. When we got off that phone call, the reality of losing my job had never been stronger.

Minutes later, it was time for my interview with Rory McIlroy, but all that was on my mind was the call with Kaitlin. Rory, meanwhile, had just had a banner day, with two eagles on his opening nine holes of play—a first for him career-wise. Once the producer sent the live coverage down to me for the interview, I immediately and unknowingly botched the question with something ridiculous like, "Rory, today was the first time you've made two birdies in nine holes in your PGA Tour career. How big was this feat?"

Like I said before, I have no problem admitting that I make mistakes, but it was never *this* kind of mistake. I sounded like a newcomer to the sport, not someone who's played it my entire life. Without skipping a beat, Rory responded as if I'd asked the question correctly and didn't take me to task for my obvious blunder. While most golf fans already know this, it's worth reiterating that Rory McIlroy is a true class act. I can't tell you how grateful I was then and still am that he didn't roast me for the error. Twitter, on the other hand, wasn't nearly as gracious. One of the nicer tweets about my question openly wondered if I had something going on because I seemed distracted. Sarcastic or not, that person hit the nail on the head. The walls were indeed starting to cave in.

A few days later, Julie Lusk reached out and asked if I wanted to meet for coffee at Starbucks, which I reluctantly agreed to do. The last thing I wanted to do was spend any amount of time with her, especially out of the office, but after all that had happened, I wanted to be able to gauge her in person. When we got together the next day, I told her that I was highly concerned because Molly knew I'd gone over her head to document my side of the story. I reminded her that it was a contract year, and I'd already seen how they appeared to be phasing me out. She promised me that my job was safe and that I had nothing to worry about. "Everybody loves you, Lisa," she assured me. "Your employee evaluations are great. Trust me; this will not affect your job." I told her it wasn't a lack of faith in her (a lie), but that she hadn't seen all the underhanded moves they continued to make. She promised me that she'd be on the lookout for anything out of the ordinary and, if necessary, HR would handle things and to notify her if the drama continued. Julie also pushed me to talk to Molly. Since Molly already knew about my conversation with Susanna and Kaitlin, it made sense for me to try to clear the air with her.

When Molly and I met in her office a few days later, her energy and attitude had changed entirely. Unlike her typical bubbly, cheerleader vibe, she'd transformed into this cold, curt person I'd never seen before. I told her the reason I'd spoken with Susanna and Kaitlin had nothing to do with her. I promised her that I wasn't trying to get anyone in trouble, but after being broadsided by the NCAA demotion and not too far removed from the Thailand drama with Mark, I felt I needed to do something to protect my livelihood. I wanted it documented, not investigated. She just sat there and listened, giving me short, simplistic answers in return.

I knew Molly was no longer on my side. Of course she wasn't. In a battle like this, who's she going to pick; her husband or me? The answer was obvious. She told me that they welcomed employees seeking to resolve issues, but her serious, political tone didn't match her message. The meeting couldn't have been more pointless.

Despite my issues with Mark, Brandel, and her husband, Molly and I had a good relationship before. She'd invited me to play golf several times, and we'd gotten together for breakfasts and lunches away from the office. And, truthfully, I enjoyed her company. But those days were long gone, and no matter what everyone kept telling me about my job security, I wasn't an idiot. I knew exactly what was coming.

As expected, things began to deteriorate rapidly. A few months later, I received an email with the second half of my yearly schedule, and my studio days were drastically reduced. Undoubtedly, after that meeting with Molly, a new game plan had been put in place. They were making a transition. By pushing me out of the building and onto the road, they were phasing me out of the studio before washing their hands of me altogether. They knew that I'd have a legal case if they didn't renew my contract without my doing something truly worthy of being fired, especially on the heels of airing my grievances with NBCUniversal's compliance office.

———————

I sent this chapter to my friend who works in HR, whom I've quoted several times in the book. After reading it, she provided this critical feedback: "It's shocking that especially someone from the legal department wouldn't inform you that they had to conduct an investigation with all involved parties. Once an employee reports an issue, the company has to look into the claims. Often it is not just about the employee in question but the potential that the same issue could impact others."

She explained that one of the main reasons companies need to investigate is to see if there's a pattern of behavior by the accused party. Also, especially when allegations of protected class violations are being levied (such as Mark Summer outing me for being gay), it's paramount to get to the root of the problem for companies to avoid litigation. When pressed for more, she added: "I doubt that [Susanna's] oversight was intentional. I can imagine her simply forgetting to tell you that compliance had a duty to question those folks you mentioned. However, if that was the case, it was incredibly stupid not to remember something so crucial. I'd be upset too if I were you."

My friend in HR also noted that most human resources personnel at these companies tend to be women. Therefore, it can be logically deduced that these female HR reps who deal with complaints like mine usually have lower status than the people they're confronting. Again, with most upper-level management positions being held predominantly by men, this consistently puts HR in a precarious position. If they genuinely work to hold powerful men accountable, they very likely could be branded "troublemakers" as well.

I asked my friend how a sexist workplace environment like Golf Channel's was allowed to persist even after decades of complaints and lawsuits. Was it HR's lack of discipline that made the place more toxic? And, if so, who were they protecting? Her answer: "If anything, human resources personnel are dealing with many of the same issues you were. It's depressing to admit, but sadly these people are often protecting their own reputations and jobs more than the employees they're supposed to be helping."

According to her, the most challenging obstacle for compliance and human resources reps to overcome is being simultaneously tasked with looking out for their company's best interests and their fellow employees' best interests. The reality is that compliance must strongly consider any legal threat to the organization and do whatever it takes to make sure they don't get sued. However, at the same time, they're supposedly there to help individuals like me who come to them when we need help. To make matters even more complicated, they're also doing everything they can to protect their own jobs. What often ends up happening is that when conflicts like mine arise, compliance and HR people end up doing little to nothing at all. They just want things to go away and worry that if they push back on the leadership, they'll suffer the same fate I did.

CHAPTER 21

THE NBC WAY

***

IF I HADN'T BEEN so desperate to talk to someone right after the blowup with Mark and Geoff in December, I undoubtedly would've done some research on Susanna before trusting her with my story. On the first page of a "Susanna Zwerling" Google search appears a Vice article where her name is mentioned several times: "NBC Couldn't Change Its Toxic Workplace Culture. But a Union Might," by Rebecca Davis, a video journalist with the network at the time.

This article was published in 2019 in response to the Matt Lauer fallout at NBC and what occurred inside 30 Rock afterward to address employees' concerns. The story's subtitle states: "After Matt Lauer's ouster, my co-workers and I tested the company's attempts at reshaping our environment. But the only thing that gave me hope was our own."

The Matt Lauer scandal had dominated the headlines, and the accompanying public fallout severely shook NBC. Rebecca and her co-workers had been subjected to NBC's obligatory apology tour from the top executives, but they worried they were still unsafe in a toxic environment. There was talk of the potential need for unionizing to protect themselves against future conflicts since there was little confidence that HR would adequately oversee it. In her article, she stated:

> "…We were called into conference rooms, 15 or so at a time, given a series of prompts about how we felt working at NBC, and told that our answers would be transcribed, anonymized, and transmitted to management. Given the heaviness in the building, the dozens more #MeToo stories that came out in newsrooms across the country in early 2018, and the six months of relative silence from higher-ups at NBC, you could guess that these efforts were met with widespread skepticism. An office full of journalists was not going to be reassured by emails and interventions that looked a lot like the bland crisis management tactics we often saw in our outside reporting…. Few of us trusted the integrity of an internal investigation, and many doubted that the new reporting channels would be any different than those currently in place."

Though their damage control people promised that things would change, it wasn't long before another public embarrassment shook the 30 Rock offices. This is also from Rebecca's article:

"The Cut had released leaked footage of NBC News journalist Chris Matthews making a rape joke about Hillary Clinton prior to an interview with her in January 2016. In the clip, as a young female associate brings what is presumably Clinton's water glass toward the set, Matthews jokes about needing a 'Bill Cosby pill' to place in the 'Queen's precious water.'"

Beyond the obvious offensiveness of Matthews' comments, after the clip went viral, NBC's human resources people once again acted as if nothing happened. This led Rebecca to reach out to Susanna Zwerling in the compliance Department.

"Hi—following up on Andy's [Andy Lack was NBC News' Chairman from 2015 to 2020] email this morning regarding NBC's desire to create a safer and more respectful environment—was curious if anything had/is being done to address this? Was deeply troubled to come across it and surprised it was never address [sic] by the company with any sort of email to employees about what action NBC was taking. Appreciate any info you may have about this matter."

Like me, Rebecca did hear back from Susanna early on, assuring her that someone would get back to her with more information about her concerns. Then a month passed with no word whatsoever. Frustrated, Rebecca sent a follow-up note, similar in tone to her previous email. This time there was no response from Susanna, or anyone else for that matter. From that day forward, no one at NBC ever contacted her about the Chris Matthews gaffe again. Matthews did publicly apologize but was never punished in any way for his offensive joke.

From Rebecca's perspective, even after being promised that the toxic masculinity problem at NBC would change, compliance and HR did little to nothing differently than they had before the Matt Lauer debacle.

On a brighter note, this motivated Rebecca and her likeminded co-workers to approach other people they knew were concerned to do the listening that Susanna and her contemporaries did not. This eventually led to NBC's digital division unionizing and beginning the long overdue process of legally advocating for a respectful, safe work environment.

Still, this poisonous behavior is far too prevalent, especially in the entertainment industry. It also illuminates how often the people hired to protect employees regularly don't do their jobs.

I recently spoke with a friend of a friend who worked at NBCUniversal during the same time I was going through my struggles at Golf Channel. Though she worked on the business end, not entertainment, she worked closely with the folks in human resources. When I asked her what her impression was of those departments back then, she shared this shocking admission: "Ironically, some of the worst people I've ever worked with were in HR."

One idea worth considering when addressing HR's seeming lack of support for so many people at NBCUniversal and Golf Channel is that maybe HR has never been an ally of the employees. After digging online, it came to my attention that since HR's inception, it was put in place by companies as a not-so-subtle public relations move and a legal buffer.

Shortly after the onset of the #MeToo movement in 2018, Sarah Lazare, a writer for InTheseTimes.com, published an article titled, "HR Has Never Been on the Side of Workers. #MeToo Is More Proof."

In the piece, Lazare wrote, "Presented as neutral arbiters, human resources departments in fact report to management and function to shield bosses from repercussions. They emerged from early anti-union efforts and social-control initiatives implemented by notorious industry titans like the Ford Motor Company—and today often house top-down efforts to undermine worker solidarity and protect companies from lawsuits."

This isn't hard to fathom when considering Ronan Farrow's reporting on NBC's history of sexual harassment cover-ups during the Matt Lauer era. However, the fact is that businesses have essentially lied to and misled their workers, telling them that HR is there to help them when they have problems with the company. If anything, their mission is the exact opposite.

With that in mind, I want to amend my earlier statement: "Often the people who are hired to protect employees don't do their jobs."

HR reps aren't there to protect employees. They're hired to protect their bosses. For that reason, Julie Lusk and Susanna Zwerling were doing their jobs just fine.

Once the dominoes started to fall, shutting me up and getting me out of the picture became their priority, too.

CHAPTER 22

REALITY HITS HOME

MAY 17, 2019. Wheels down at XNA, the regional airport in Northwest Arkansas. In all the years I'd lived away from home, it's the only time I can ever recall not being excited to be there. This was a trip I'd been dreading since receiving the scheduling email five months prior.

The last time I was in my hometown wasn't too far removed from this day. I'd been asked by someone in Golf Channel's public relations department if I'd be willing to emcee the on-site media day ahead of the NCAA championships and do a session with reporters afterward. At the time, he had no idea that I'd been demoted to the reporter's role and was just trying to get the week over with and off my mind as quickly as possible. The last thing I wanted to do was say yes to his request, but I've always liked and respected this person and he really wanted me to be there because of my connection to the area, so I said yes. I also never wanted to give Molly or Geoff any opportunity to say that I stopped doing what was asked of me. Saying no would've actually been easy since, in order to arrive on time that

Monday, I had to fly overnight on a red eye after the conclusion of a tournament I was working the previous week on the West Coast.

I don't remember too many details from that day except changing clothes in the airport bathroom and the effort it took to put a smile on my face as best as I could once I arrived at the course where the session with the local media was taking place. I gave some BS interview with a reporter about how excited I was for the NCAA championships to be in my hometown and how it was such an honor to represent Golf Channel, which was nothing short of a big, fat lie. Molly must've been shocked when she learned that I actually said positive things in the article about the network, given all that had happened in the last several months. I must admit that I was equally stunned when she emailed me the day after the article was published: "Lisa, so much terrific coverage of you and the Arkansas program. Great job representing us. Can't wait for the week."

The workweek for the tournament began like any other, with a production meeting the day before coverage was scheduled to start. Ironically, as the only hometown person on the main crew for the event, I was also the only person who was late for the meeting because I got lost. My GPS directed me to the wrong location of our makeshift production compound. When I arrived several minutes late, the live tournament producer made some snide remark about me showing up whenever I wanted to. I just smiled and waved, not paying much attention to it. Then he went through the assignments and plans for the next few days. Fifteen minutes later, we were out of there—no one more eager to leave than me.

After the meeting, I went to the practice facilities to say hi to some players, coaches, and Razorbacks golf support staff. The first two people I ran into were the Arkansas women's head coach and a longtime member of the sports information department, both of whom are good friends. They'd already heard the news that I wasn't hosting and wanted to know why, especially this year. I gave them the abbreviated version of the story and told them the situation with

Golf Channel wasn't good—that some things were going on behind the scenes, all of which made me believe my job was in jeopardy. They were both baffled by this revelation and asked if there was anything they could do. "Unfortunately not," I told them. I think they were in shock, given my history with the network and knowing my role had continued to climb until that point. I didn't have the time or the energy to tell them the whole story—that my role started dwindling when I called Brandel to the carpet with Molly's husband. It was such a twisted, messed-up chain of events with many layers to it, and I knew they had more important things to focus on at the moment. But I made them both a promise that the entire story would come out one day. We shared hugs and said our goodbyes. Their words of encouragement gave me a big boost at a time when I needed it the most.

The next day I put those emotions aside and was in reporter mode. I came into the round with ideas about some stories I wanted to tell on the course. Considering I was new to this particular role, I wasn't exactly sure what to expect. Covering college golf is much different from professional golf since it's a team environment with a coach. Without much direction going in, I waited for the producer to guide me where he wanted me to be to conduct any in-play or post-round interviews. I was trying to follow his lead as much as possible since I wasn't as familiar with the role. It all seemed to be going okay until an hour or so into the broadcast when I pitched him the idea of a story I wanted to share about the head coach at Auburn, whose mom just so happens to be Dale McNamara, my former coach at Tulsa.

Melissa McNamara (now Luellen) was a great player in her own right, winning the individual national title in 1988 when she was playing for her mom at TU. Dale was out there that day in Fayetteville watching her daughter's team, so the synergy was perfect. I told him what I wanted to do over the headset, and he agreed to send the coverage to me as soon as possible. So I sat there in my cart and waited... and waited...and waited. I checked in with him at the 10-minute mark. "Working on it," he said. Then again, after another 10 minutes, still nothing. When he went to break shortly after, I reminded him that I was sitting there waiting to share this story and missing out on other action because of the delay. Nearly 40 minutes after my initial request, he finally sent the coverage to me so I could talk about Dale and Melissa. The apparent snub was frustrating, but I kept going. *Maybe this is my punishment for being late to the meeting,* I thought to myself. Half joking, half serious.

As the week went on, I interviewed many other coaches and players, but the interview that meant the most to me was with Haley Moore's dad, Tom. Haley was a senior at the University of Arizona at the time, and her team had won the national title the year prior. Haley made the final putt that week to secure the championship. It was a great moment that was celebrated across the sport. Since then, she's been very open about being bullied throughout her life. Haley's a towering presence with a gentle soul and has also been forthcoming about her struggles with weight issues over the years. It still amazes me how cruel human beings can sometimes be to each other.

Her dad and I discussed what she'd been through on-air and how making that putt gave Haley even more confidence off the golf course than it did on it. It was a memorable two minutes we shared and one of my favorite interviews in all my years as a broadcaster.

Later that week, when I was back in Orlando, I received an email from Molly that included the following:

> I thought you would have contributed more to the tournament broadcast—being aggressive with getting coach interviews or relatives during play on Tuesday and early wednesday, adding some informational nuggets on players or families. Make sure to get with the producer and talk about expectations, etc. next time in advance. I've spoken to Brandt [the producer], too.

I know you were disappointed in the NCAA women's role. My hope is that you are putting it behind you and working hard on your GC team relationships and roles for the summer.

This was the most Molly email ever. The first thing I thought to myself was, *Did she even fucking watch?* There was always a running joke around Golf Channel that she indeed never did watch. That joke just proved itself to be a reality with her email. Players. Coaches. Families. Storytelling. I did as much of it as I possibly could that week. Then there was the "my hope is that you are putting it behind you and working hard on your GC team relationships" comment, which couldn't have been more out of touch. Why didn't she just say Brandel, since that was the only relationship that needed mending—and one that I asked her husband to assist with, which led to all of this in the first place?

Not long after the previously discussed blow-up with Geoff over Brandel, Molly told my agent, "She really needs to learn how to get along with Brandel since he's our lead analyst." Molly and Geoff didn't care about what was right. They cared about protecting the assets they wanted to be protected. Nothing more.

By this time, my internal antenna was way up on Molly and her husband, and I was paying close attention to everything. Not only did she completely ignore the quality stories and reporting I did that week, but she also made sure to call into question my ability to get along with my co-workers, which most would say couldn't have been further from the truth. I got along with everyone except the men who were closest to her.

My guess is she wanted all of this laid out in an email so she could start building her case for what was to come. But there was a significant problem for her: my yearly evaluations from Mark Summer, which she no doubt had to sign off on. Here's a portion of his feedback as it pertains to the last words in her email:

Lisa is a great ambassador for Golf Channel and she's always requested to make appearances. It's been a pleasure working with Lisa over the past 12 months and I look forward to Lisa continuing to grow in 2018. Lisa is a good people person, very easy to work with and get along with.

Molly was building her case on nothing more than falsehoods and inaccuracies that she and Geoff had created. Meanwhile, I had receipts just like this…and a lot of them.

CHAPTER 23

THE UNTOUCHABLES

WITH THE WEEK in Arkansas for NCAAs finally behind me, it was time to head back to Orlando. When I sat down at the departure gate at XNA, I passed the time the way I usually do…by unproductively scrolling through my Twitter feed. That's when I saw a couple of comments from a co-worker named Matt Ginella that were impossible to ignore.

Golf Channel hired Matt in 2013 as a travel insider to give recaps of trips he'd taken (on the company dime) to the best golf vacation spots on the planet. Golf Channel's website described him this way: "Ginella provides viewers with tips and advice for their golf travel, both in the United States and around the world. In addition to his on-air work, Ginella is a senior editor for GolfAdvisor.com. Before joining Golf Channel, Ginella was a senior travel editor for Golf Digest and Golf World magazines."

Referring to the chapter addressing nepotism, the common story at Golf Channel was that Matt had this high-profile, high-paying job because of his longtime friendship with Molly and Geoff. Truthfully, it wasn't something I cared about too much because I rarely worked with Matt. We did host a couple of events together over the years, and I was well aware beforehand that he had a bit of an ego and loved having the spotlight on him. So I let him do his thing. It was fine, no big deal.

What he was doing on this particular day, however, wasn't fine at all. It involved my old friend and fellow Arkansan, John Daly. As most golf fans know, since the early 1990s, John's been a flamboyant, larger-than-life figure—famous for his monstrous drives and wild antics on and off the course. Affectionately nicknamed "Wild Thing," he's known for poking holes in golf's stuffy country club culture. Safe to say, he's also far from perfect, and John would be the first to admit it. In my opinion, his brutal honesty is one of his most endearing qualities.

John's long been notorious for his wild-man, party-animal lifestyle. This has led to attempts at rehabilitation from alcohol abuse, multiple turbulent marriages, on-course meltdowns, and legal troubles. In his 2016 ESPN-produced documentary *Hit It Hard,* John admitted that he played numerous PGA Tour events hungover, even copping to a solitary instance of one mid-round binge at an official event. During the L.A. Open (now the Genesis Invitational), John told ESPN, "It was so slow, and I played the back nine first. I think I'm two or three over. I went to the locker room and downed like five beers, and I think I shot four under on the front nine. That is the only time I know I drank during a round, and I played great. I played great that week. I finished strong."

This type of unapologetic bravado has endeared John to many, and it also inevitably polarizes more straightlaced, reverential people. Since that same buttoned-up personality type is prevalent among the gatekeepers of the golf world, the *Hit It Hard* documentary probably created as many naysayers as it did fans. But that's nothing John isn't used to in his life and career. He lives large, swings for the fences, and gives everyone in attendance a real show. Say what you will about his personality, his golf game is equal parts marvelous and supremely entertaining.

In a career that's spanned more than 30 years, through numerous personal and professional highs and lows, John's continued to be a beloved character and a huge draw on the PGA Tour. Even now, playing primarily on the PGA Tour Champions, he regularly pulls larger galleries than the tournament leaders. In that way, John's a lot like Tiger Woods. No matter where they stand on the leaderboard, the circus still follows.

I've always had a huge soft spot for John, partly because we have several things in common. For starters, when John was four, his family moved from Carmichael, California, to Dardanelle, Arkansas, where my dad was born and raised. Like me, when John was in high school, he won the Arkansas State Amateur Championship. In college, he attended the University of Arkansas and played for the Razorbacks men's golf team. But I think the thing I identify most with JD about is that we've never been afraid to tell it like it is, even when it probably would've been wiser to stay silent. We call people out when we see improprieties, and we both take credit for our mistakes when we make them. We make up for what we lack in filters with guts, tenacity, and a genuine concern for others.

I first met John at a charity golf tournament when I was a teenager at the top of my game. We ended up playing a few holes together and immediately hit it off. John had already won his first of two major championships and was a rock star wherever he went. When he told me that day that he'd been reading about my success and was pulling for me, it was like Elvis saying that to a promising young musician. Although I rooted for John long before we met, now that I know him personally, it's grown into this feeling like he's a member of my extended family. That's how Arkansans often are with each other. And no matter what anyone else thinks of him, John Daly is good for golf. Even the controversy he sometimes generates puts golf on a larger stage. Following the fallout that came with John's *Hit It Hard* revelations, I knew it was only a matter of time before golf's gatekeepers found another reason to try to come down on him.

During the lead-up to the 2019 PGA Championship, John was again embroiled in a divisive position. As a past champion, thanks to his win in 1991 at Crooked Stick, he has a lifetime exemption into the PGA Championship. By 2019, it'd been 15 years since he'd won a PGA Tour event, let alone a third major, but (barring injuries) John would always show up ready to compete every year. The problem in 2019 was that he'd also applied for a highly controversial medical exemption: he wanted to be allowed to drive a golf cart during the championship. Considering the staggering length and tiring terrain of the host course, Bethpage Black, there was little doubt he could compete without it.

A few months before the PGA Championship, word started to spread that John had applied for the cart exemption, citing osteoarthritis in his right knee as the reason. Not long after, the PGA of America ruled in his favor, granting him the right to use the cart. When pressed for answers as to why, the PGA of America confirmed that he was covered under the Americans with Disabilities Act. Still not satisfied, the media and his detractors laid into him publicly, questioning his sincerity and declaring it an indictment on the integrity of the game itself. Tiger Woods even got in on the ribbing. Referring to his legendarily gritty win at the 2008 U.S. Open at a Tuesday presser at Bethpage, Tiger jabbed: "Well, I walked with a broken leg, so…" John responded seriously, lamenting that he wished Woods had "all the facts" before making light of his situation.

"Might have been a different comment," he told USA Today Sports, "as well as Golf Channel Wednesday morning when they bashed me pretty good, and a few others who criticized me…. Osteoarthritis is a tough thing, brother. If my knee was broke[n], I would have had it fixed. But my situation is totally different. It's painful as hell is all I can say. As was Tiger's, I'm sure."

Regardless of my friendship with John, I still couldn't understand why everyone was so up in arms about him using a cart. No one thought he was going to win the PGA Championship that year. PGA Tour pros in their physical primes were mowed down in waves that week. Bethpage Black is hands down one of the most demanding golf courses on the planet. John was a past champion who was due the honor of being allowed to play, but more importantly, he was a certifiably disabled person who was asking for his constitutionally protected civil right. The PGA of America agreed with him.

With the 2019 PGA Championship wrapping up the weekend prior, John was still taking plenty of shots from Golf Twitter for riding in a cart during the event. Of all the critics who were attacking John, the one who stood out to me well above the others was Matt Ginella. On that day, sitting at the airport, I couldn't believe what he was tweeting publicly about John. You can't do that as a journalist, and you shouldn't do it regardless, especially using words that were so defamatory. In response to a tweet that read, "No one has ever used a cart in the history of @TheOpen," Matt replied via quote tweet:

> This story of Daly using a cart at majors must end now. He's sad. The fact he was able to use a cart at the @PGAChampionship was pathetic. [Brooks] Koepka, an athlete, winning a major at Bethpage in May was two steps forward. Daly competing in a cart was a step back for golf and the @PGA.

Not only were his words harsh and completely disrespectful, but his remarks also blindly disregarded John's legitimate disability diagnosis. Taking a quick scroll through the comment threads, it was no surprise that Matt's hot take wasn't landing as he'd hoped. When a follower sarcastically asked, "Matt, hello. Why does this matter at all?" Ginella clapped back rhetorically:

> Hmmm…this really needs an explanation? It portrays the game in the worst light. It does a disservice to the professionals who take their jobs seriously. It's enabling an underachiever and I want the next generation of golfers to know that's not what they should aspire to.

At that point, I couldn't help but weigh in on the debate. After the week I'd just had, any previous concern I may have had for what Molly and Geoff or their people might think of me challenging another one of their golden boys was out the window. I was incensed and didn't hesitate when I quote tweeted his "underachiever" reply with this:

> Pretty harsh labeling a two-time major winner an "underachiever," Matt. Like him or not – John Daly has played a big role in growing the game over the years.

Within minutes Matt fired back:

> He won them while drinking. He's definitely an underachiever. I chose my words carefully.

I was a bit taken aback by his annoyance in that remark and the fact that he wasn't backing down or taking ownership of crossing the line with his words regarding John. While I strongly disagreed with his thoughts on the Daly cart issue, I thought my reply was nothing more than typical Twitter fodder. So I countered with:,

> He won them while drinking. What in the world does that mean?

Seconds later, from Matt:

> I sent you a direct message and a link that explains what in
> the world that means.

Now things seemed to be getting oddly personal. I went straight
to my inbox, where Matt's reply was waiting for me.

> Lisa, Daly is a disgrace. You were there when he walked off
> the Pure Insurance because he didn't want to wait on the
> second tee. Meanwhile, Watson, Irwin, Kite…they all waited.
> A tournament that includes First Tee kids. On the drinking:

What followed was a link that directed me to one of many stories
detailing John's comments about slamming beers in the L.A. Open
that were in the *Hit It Hard* documentary. Without bothering to re-
read what I already knew to be true, I decided it was time to explain
to Matt why I cared enough about John to take up for him publicly.

> I've read one hundred articles just like that. I also know
> John very well. You say you choose your words carefully –
> perhaps you could try harder. John is not a disgrace. Has
> he done disgraceful things? Yes. He is a very flawed person
> who has failed publicly and privately over the years. But he
> also is a man who keeps trying to be better. He's a fantastic
> father. Has been overly generous with his time and his giv-
> ing over the years. If you knew him, you would never call
> him a disgrace. You would pull for him to keep trying to be
> better. To try to share with people that he is so much more
> than the flawed human being we've seen over the years. He
> still works at his game and wants to be better. It's okay to
> question his motivation. But to label him as a person based

on his public shortcomings isn't fair. He's a much better person than people know. We (live) in a very judgmental world unfortunately. And judgment like that does nothing to make anything better. This is also a very judgmental game. Let's be honest…if John was an Ivy League educated, good looking guy with a clean past, this whole cart issue (because he truly has a degenerative disease) wouldn't be as big a deal.

Within a minute or two of my reply, Matt immediately had another rebuttal:

John Daly shouldn't have competed in the PGA in a cart. He took advantage of the situation. I'm so glad you like John Daly, and he has given you so much time, but that's not my issue. You're defending him, that's fine, a noble effort. I'm defending the game of golf.

That's where his message to me ended, and the following words from Twitter picked up: YOU CAN NO LONGER SEND DIRECT MESSAGES TO THIS PERSON.

I couldn't believe what I was seeing. Matt Ginella had just blocked me over a debate about John Daly using a cart. *You have to be kidding me,* I thought. It didn't even feel like we were arguing. From my standpoint, it seemed like a worthy discussion. At this point, I was so over the continued haughty antics by these protected antagonists at Golf Channel that I fired back publicly after snapping a screenshot showing Matt Ginella had blocked me, adding these words above the image:

I just got BLOCKED by a co-worker for having a difference of opinion on the John Daly cart issue. This thin-skinned world in which we live needs to toughen up.

Okay, I'll admit that may not have been my most tempered and professional reaction. But, immediately, my screenshot tweet started lighting up, with the overwhelming sentiment being that Matt Ginella was a pompous jerk. I also began noticing screenshots from people who were posting on my comments showing trolls slamming Matt's tweet that bashed Daly. They kept asking him why he'd block a co-worker just for having a different viewpoint on a reasonably small issue. In Twitterspeak, he was being ratioed. The public sentiment on the Daly tweet by Matt went from mixed to overwhelmingly negative. I'd just killed two Ginella tweets with one stone. It felt like justice.

Not long after my tweet had gone viral, I received a message from Matt's longtime protector, Geoff Russell, asking me to call him. He sternly informed me that I needed to talk to Matt. Geoff was upset because my screenshot tweet left a digital record online that would never go away. He said it would've been fine if it'd all happened on air versus online, which made little sense. Not surprisingly, he didn't mention Matt being out of line with his words toward John. I told him I was okay to talk to Matt because the entire situation was silly. He'd cut off the communication, not me. It also wasn't surprising that I was the one who had to step up and send the email to Ginella, which I copied Geoff on. Matt replied that he'd always respected my work and would unblock me. As expected, Geoff never mentioned it again or responded to my email.

Within minutes of our public Twitter feud, I started getting texts from some co-workers. The most eyebrow-raising of them all was: "I can't stand him so I'm all for you burying him. Just don't get called into the principal's office. He's untouchable."

I responded, "Geoff already text[ed] us both together. You should read the stuff Matt said…telling me he's covered the game for 24 years. Blah, blah, blah. He's an insecure little boy."

His reply: "BARF."

"I have no doubt I'll be asked to take that post down," I replied, "which I will as soon as he acknowledges that he shouldn't have blocked a co-worker…He's a joke and knows nothing about the game."

A one-word mic drop, again: "Untouchable."

"Well, I'm clearly not untouchable," I conceded, "I wonder If Turner is hiring?"

"You're our best reporter," he responded. "Like not even in the same stratosphere as the rest."

From that moment on, whether I wanted it or not, Matt Ginella was an enemy. Also, thanks to the fact that the entire office knew about our Twitter feud, many of my co-workers came to me privately, telling me how much they despised Ginella and thanked me for exposing him as the fraud they thought he was. I heard stories of bullying, disgusting sexist behavior, and all types of retaliatory actions. A good friend of mine who worked with Matt and Geoff during their time at *Golf World* said that back then, word around the office was that Matt was a sleazy, lecherous jerk. For example, at a staff meeting, in front of a table full of fellow employees, Matt was witnessed shamelessly hitting on a female co-worker. The comments included something to the effect of how hot she looked and creepily complimenting her outfit. My friend said everyone in the room was visibly cringing and uncomfortable throughout the interaction.

Most of the people I've spoken with who have horror stories about Matt are afraid to go on record due to fear of retaliation from Molly and Geoff. But one of his own *Golf Digest* stories published in 2011 does a strong job demonstrating the enabling and encouragement of Matt's sexism. It's a piece titled, "Q&A: Catching up with Tiffany, Tips from The Beverage Cart Girl."

The article starts by referencing an earlier slideshow on GolfDigest. com called "The 18 Most Annoying Golf Partners." After declaring it to be one of the most popular features that has ever run on their website, Matt goes on to attribute a large chunk of its popularity to the fact that the slideshow also featured Tiffany, a sexy young model who posed for the slideshow shoot in a low-cut top that revealed her large breasts. Posed and shot in a leering way, the photos of Tiffany come off more like something straight out of a Maxim magazine than a respected golf publication.

From the very beginning of the interview, Matt lets the reader in on the alleged joke, that this is all lighthearted, self-aware misogyny masquerading as hot doggery. He tells his readers: "Because I love you, I was able to get my hands on a few extra photos [of Tiffany] and a behind the scenes video of the shoot."

"I called Tiffany for a quick Q&A," Matt begins the interview. "(It's my job. It's what I do.)"

Matt: "As a beverage cart girl, have you been subject to marriage proposals?"

Tiffany: "I think there was probably one in there. I get a lot of vacation offers. And other requests."

Soon after, Matt asks, "Can you give the readers some tips on how a guy might flirt with a beverage cart girl and potentially walk away with a phone number?"

Tiffany: "Just say, 'Hey, I enjoyed talking to you. I'm sure you get told this all the time, but you seem interesting, would you like to hang out?' Something like that. Be subtle."

Matt: "People are going to want to know, are you single?"

Tiffany: "Yes, you can say I'm single."

Matt: "Hey listen, I enjoyed talking to you. I'm sure you get this all the time, but you seem interesting, would you like to hang out?"

This wouldn't be the last time that Matt Ginella and I had a heated exchange on Twitter. What changed after he blocked me, though, was that I could now see how the web of Molly and Geoff's untouchable friends were coming at me from different directions.

Like a cryptic puzzle, many of the pieces didn't seem to fit together for a while. But once my lawyer began his discovery process for our EEOC case, all of those disjointed pieces started to come together.

CHAPTER 24

DEMOTED

SO FAR, **2019** had already been a roller coaster ride emotionally, but I didn't realize it was just a warmup compared to what
would come next. It was September 18, to be exact, and I'd arrived in
Australia the day prior—straight from covering the Solheim Cup in
Scotland. Molly was at the event that week, but I only saw her once.
It was an accidental run-in in the hallway of the hotel where we were
staying. She seemed uncomfortable when we bumped into each other
and was almost at a loss for words. She apologized for having to rush
away quickly, telling me she had to get to "a meeting." I could sense
that something was off immediately. Fast-forward four or five days
later and that brief encounter, as concerning as it felt then, was the
furthest thing from my mind. This was the day I was going to ask Sarah
to marry me. I was so incredibly nervous but also blissfully happy.

When I woke up that morning, I could feel my stomach churning.
I'd had this day planned out in my mind for a while. We were going
to play golf at her home course, New South Wales Golf Club, located
right on the edge of the Pacific Ocean. The views there are stunning,

especially looking down the par-5 5th hole with the waves splashing against the rocks. That's where it was going to happen.

After playing the scene out in my head, I glanced at my phone and noticed there was a missed call from my agent. I'd been expecting to hear from him at some point that week since my contract was up at the end of the year, and this was typically the time when we'd get the renewal offer. Gregg knew I was in Australia and left a voicemail for me to call him. Like most agents, he isn't one to put off the inevitable and got right to the point when I called him back. "Lisa, I can't believe I have to tell you this…" he said. "I finally talked to Molly early this morning, and the offer for next year is only a part-time, freelance reporting position. When I asked her for an explanation, all she could tell me was she was sorry, but because of budget issues, that's all she could offer. Ten weeks guaranteed but nothing more and no studio days." Gregg and I talked for a few more minutes. He tried his best to be encouraging and said we'd figure this out but to try to enjoy my time in Australia and to call him as soon as I got home.

Sarah, not knowing that I'd just gone from the ultimate high of thinking about our future together to the realization of my career ending at Golf Channel in the span of two short minutes, looked at me in a way that I could tell she was concerned. She'd heard the conversation with Gregg and was ready for what I was about to say.

"They're pushing me out. I told you they've been preparing for this for a while. It all makes sense now. The reduced studio days, NCAAs… everything. She's giving me 10 weeks, so it doesn't look like I'm being let go. Companies do this when they want to get rid of someone with a good track record so they don't get sued. I guarantee you this will be the last offer I ever get from Molly…and I promise you, I won't let her or her husband get away with everything they've done."

Somehow, I was able to put all of that aside so we could celebrate the day, which still ended up being the best day of my life. But I meant what I said to Sarah in the hotel room that morning. I was already mentally preparing for the fight of my life.

When we got home a week or so later, I was back at work immediately. The first day in the building after learning my fate was hard. I felt like a member of the walking dead. As much as I loathed some of the higher-ups like Molly and Geoff, there were so many people at Golf Channel I cared for deeply, and the thought of not working with them anymore was heartbreaking. I told those I was closest to about my fate, and we all shared some somber moments together. But then there was the other side of me—the angry side. I wasn't surprised that Molly hadn't reached out. Any normal human being would've felt some sort of remorse. But Molly isn't like most human beings in that regard. Once she no longer has a purpose for you, you no longer matter.

Determined to make her give me some explanations to my face, I emailed her assistant to set up a meeting, which she did for later that week. In typical Molly fashion, on the day of our scheduled meeting, she had her assistant email me and tell me that she needed to push back the time and, if it was more convenient for me, she could call me instead of meeting in person. *No thanks,* I replied, making it clear that I wanted a face-to-face meeting, not a phone call. So we rescheduled.

When we finally did meet in person, I broke down in her office. I was furious but also deeply hurt. I'd done everything she—or anyone else I reported to, for that matter—had asked me to do during the entire time I worked there. I came into work on my days off, filled in when there were scheduling conflicts, had gone on media day shoots when I wasn't even supposed to be working, said yes to every appearance request—absolutely everything. The only thing I didn't do was cower down to Chamblee, Ginella, and Molly's power-hungry husband, Geoff Russell. In almost six years, I'd gone from an eager new employee who was beyond thrilled to be working for this woman to the realization that *this woman* had become the greatest disappointment of my professional career. That afternoon would be the last time I ever talked to Molly Solomon.

CHAPTER 25

DECISIONS

***

ON **SEPTEMBER 29,** 2019, I sent the following text to a former co-worker:

> I just wanted to say thank you again for coming over last night. I can't begin to tell you how much that meant and will always mean to me. You've been a voice of reason during this rocky road I've been on lately. It says a lot about you as a person and a co-worker to be there when needed. I will always be a fan…and grateful for that.

The day before I sent him that text would become an important date in my case against Golf Channel. Before then, I was 90 percent sure I wanted to talk to a lawyer. After that day, there was no doubt remaining whatsoever.

Once word started getting around that I was being relegated to a part-time, freelance reporter at the network, many people I worked with started reaching out to show their support, including the person I sent the text to that night. He'd gotten wind that a few other co-workers were coming to my house and wanted to stop by to make sure I was doing okay and lend his support as well. This was something he'd done on several occasions over the years both in person and on the phone. While he was there, he told me about a recent encounter he'd had with Brandel. When the conversation began, he assumed I already knew about it, given how quickly word travels and how loose Brandel was with his words the night they were together. When I told him I didn't have the faintest idea what he was talking about, he proceeded to tell me the entire story.

He and two other co-workers, plus one of their friends who didn't work at Golf Channel, were all having dinner together at a restaurant in Winter Park—a suburb just north of Orlando. Brandel was sitting at the bar when he spotted the four of them at a table and came over and sat down. He said he could tell as soon as the conversation began that Brandel had had a few drinks. After a few minutes of small talk and entirely out of the blue, the producer's friend asked Brandel, "Hey, why do people think you're such an asshole on TV?" Brandel went into how much he prepares for each show and has no problem speaking his mind, which people often don't like. Then, Brandel quickly (and oddly, my co-worker added) shifted gears to me. He said something about him being the exact opposite of me—someone who was never prepared and not good at my job and, most notably, that he'd been after Molly for the last year or two to get rid of me because I wasn't a good representative of Golf Channel.

His last admission was the final piece of the puzzle. Brandel Chamblee. Matt Ginella. Geoff Russell. They all had something in common: significant influence over Molly. It didn't matter that I had a great relationship with her. What mattered was that I had run-ins with the three men she was closest with at the network. And since Molly so desperately wanted to be liked by these particular men, she gave them what they wanted when I became their collective enemy. If you were a woman who spoke out, this was your fate. Less than a year later, the same scenario would become Chantel McCabe's fate, too. Although she's never spoken about it publicly, she faced her own bouts of backlash from Brandel, which (as previously mentioned) led to him childishly blocking her on Twitter for no reason, just as he'd done with me. There were many instances of unfair treatment toward Chantel at Golf Channel, but that's her story to tell, not mine. I'll just say that she was good at her job and shouldn't have been replaced because she refused to get pushed around.

Within a day or two, I reached out to a local lawyer I knew reasonably well through a couple of friends at work. We'd all played golf together many times over the years, so I felt completely comfortable telling him a little about what had happened on the phone and asked if we could talk in person. I wanted to know my options.

Without hesitation, he agreed and arranged for us to meet at Isleworth Country Club on a specific day the following week. We met in a small conference room upstairs, where I told him the entire story. He took detailed notes, asked relevant questions, and was fully engaged. After laying out his legal analysis in response, I was surprised by how quickly he concluded that this would be a challenging case to try and to win. Plus, it would be expensive. Considering how enthused I'd been before our meeting, his assessment of my situation left me discouraged, to say the least. But there was no way I was giving up just yet.

That night, I called my cousin Allison to share the news with her. Allison is not only one of the closest people in my life, but she's an exceptional lawyer. Unfortunately, she's a tax lawyer, so this type of case is out of her realm of experience. Like me, Allison was disappointed when she heard his reaction. But also, like me, she wasn't deterred. We talked about it for a little bit, and then I asked her about a lawyer she knows well who handles discrimination cases. I thought maybe she could give me some advice as to where to turn next. Allison agreed it was a good idea and asked the lawyer if she'd be willing to talk to me. She said she would and wanted to know if I'd be in Little Rock anytime soon. It just so happened that I was going to be there in a couple of weeks. With all the painful and problematic issues taking place in my work life at the time, something special was about to happen in my personal life. I was being inducted into the Arkansas State Golf Association Hall of Fame.

Two days after the induction ceremony, Allison took Sarah and me to her friend's house, where we all convened around the dining table just off the kitchen. There was some light talk for a few minutes before she said in a serious tone, "Okay, let's hear it. Tell me everything." Having Sarah and Allison there to help answer questions and give their sides of the story was a huge benefit. Like the previous lawyer, she took pages of notes and asked many pertinent questions. Unlike the last meeting, however, she was engaged as a lawyer but also as a woman. She would often gasp or shake her head in disbelief at what she was hearing. After revealing every detail, she was unwavering in her opinion—not only did I have a strong case, I had a winnable case. All I needed was the right lawyer to represent me. She asked me to give her a few days to think about it, and she'd be back in touch. There was no hesitation at all. You could hear the determination in her voice. This stoic woman had taken my hope, which had been on life support, and suddenly breathed new life into me.

PART V

FIRING BACK

————

CHAPTER 26

ENTER TOM MARS

IT DIDN'T TAKE the lawyer my cousin connected me with very long at all to come back with a name. A few days after our meeting, Sarah and I were back home in Orlando playing golf one morning when my phone rang. It was Allison on the other end. She started the conversation by telling me they had the perfect person in mind to take my case.

"Have you heard of Tom Mars?" Allison asked.

"No," I replied.

"Do you remember Houston Nutt's case against Ole Miss?" She followed up.

"The one that exposed Hugh Freeze as a bible-thumping phony who was calling prostitutes on his work cell phone? Of course, I do. I know it well," I quickly answered.

"Well, Tom was Houston's lawyer," she said back.

For a few seconds, there was complete silence. So many thoughts were running through my head. I'd read all about Tom Mars—the person who almost single-handedly took down the Ole Miss football program—and they wanted him to represent me. Now all they had to do was convince their former colleague to take the case.

The Tale of Tom Mars reads like any true epic biography. Tom grew up in the suburbs of Washington, D.C., dreaming of becoming an FBI agent. As a young man, he worked as a police officer in Virginia before changing course and attending law school. In true Tom fashion, he barely passed the LSAT and then finished first in his law school class. After making the top score on the bar exam, he accepted an offer to practice at the esteemed Rose Law Firm in Little Rock, reporting directly to Hillary Rodham Clinton. He would later become the director of the Arkansas State Police and a member of Arkansas Governor Mike Huckabee's cabinet. Continuing to climb the legal ranks, in 2002, Tom was hired by Wal-Mart Stores, Inc., where he served seven years as general counsel and four years as the company's chief administrative officer. During his time with Wal-Mart, Tom led an ambitious diversity initiative and became a nationally known champion for advancing diversity in the legal profession.

In 2020, following his high-profile clobbering of Ole Miss in the protected world of college football, the *Wall Street Journal* featured Tom in its September edition, recalling his first legal triumph while working at the Rose Law Firm: "[Tom's] first major case was a successful class action in a natural gas deal against a business that was co-owned by Dallas Cowboys owner Jerry Jones." Tom doggedly battled Jones' lawyers, winning the suit in slam-dunk fashion with a verdict of more than 17 million dollars. The WSJ went on to add that "Jerry was so impressed by the lawyer who whupped him that he invited Tom onto the [Cowboys] field for a game. 'I didn't like any part of that case, Tom,' Tom recalls Jerry telling him later, 'but you did a hell of a job.'"

In the battle with Ole Miss, again in typical Tom fashion, he jokes that going in he knew absolutely nothing about college football. By his own admission, he had very little interest in taking the case when the former 'SEC Coach of the Year' first contacted him. Still, he agreed to meet Nutt in person and listen to him explain how his reputation was being slandered by new Ole Miss head coach Hugh Freeze and the higher-ups at the University.

What was at the center of Houston Nutt's claims? First, after Nutt was fired by the school in 2016, the NCAA notified Ole Miss that it was being served a Notice of Allegations (NOA) alleging numerous and exceedingly serious rule violations within the Ole Miss football program. These violations included bribing recruits with money and improper gifts, academic fraud, and more. When the NOA was first made public on the eve of Ole Miss' biggest recruiting event of the year, the school—including Ole Miss chancellor Ross Bjork—privately told sportswriters that almost all of the football team's violations had happened during Nutt's head coaching reign.

Soon after, the national sportswriters who were misled by the school's misinformation campaign published numerous news stories portraying Nutt as the orchestrator of the egregious rule violations. These misleading stories also conveyed the false impression to Ole Miss recruits that the NCAA investigation wouldn't tarnish its football program or Hugh Freeze's self-made reputation as a faith-based, trustworthy leader of young men.

It's worth noting that Coach Nutt wasn't seeking a financial settlement from Ole Miss. All he wanted was an apology from the school and a clarification. Specifically, the clarification was to spell out that while there were allegations of misconduct during his tenure, most of the allegations in the NOA weren't related to him. He claimed that the heightened negative publicity and innuendo had hurt his family (including his elderly mother) and were keeping the 59-year-old coach from finding another job.

Since his early police days and FBI training, Tom had taught himself how to dig deep and uncover any potential evidence that could prove to be beneficial. He never cut corners or gave up easily. He visited and revisited every possible lead. Also, having served as general counsel for the biggest company in the world, he trained his body and his mind to commit as many hours as necessary to get the job done. This combination makes Tom a brilliant lawyer—an investigative genius with an unwavering work ethic.

Once Tom took Nutt's case, his endgame was evident: unearth the truth at Ole Miss and clear Nutt's name. He began working 15-hour days, seven days a week. Soon, a trusted ally would connect him with Steve Robertson, a reporter for a fan website devoted to rival school Mississippi State. Robertson had spent his professional career digging dirt on the Rebels and fearlessly fighting Ole Miss fans online. When Tom learned of his tenacious reputation, he reached out to Robertson. The two men formed an unlikely alliance that would eventually unwind a twisted conspiracy that went all the way up the chain of command to Ole Miss' new head football coach and top administrative brass.

Both keen investigators, they admittedly obsessed over their detective work. After countless hours of meticulous research, Robertson scored the most significant break while scouring through Hugh Freeze's cell phone records, which Tom obtained through the Freedom of Information Act. Amid mostly useless information, Robertson came across one number that stood out. When he plugged the number into Google out of curiosity and a strong hunch, he couldn't believe what it revealed. Hugh Freeze, a devout Christian who often spoke publicly about his faith and service to the Lord, had called an escort service on a University-issued cell phone. That call log was the smoking gun.

When Tom confronted Ole Miss about it, Freeze said it was a misdial. But, as Tom still explains to this day, "What do you do if you call a wrong number? You call back." Of course, there weren't any return calls to a similar number. Tom knew Freeze was lying and announced his findings to the press. After a deeper investigation, the school discovered a pattern of misconduct when Freeze traveled—hiring prostitutes through various escort services.

Within weeks of the school's internal investigation, Freeze was fired as the head football coach, and soon after, Ole Miss issued a public apology to Houston Nutt and settled the lawsuit. Even worse, the University faced sanctions from the NCAA, including being deemed ineligible for the upcoming season's bowl games. Tom had just taken on Goliath and won with nothing but a small bag of perfectly aimed stones. In Tom's own words, "This was a smear campaign. If it weren't so deceitful and morally wrong, it would probably go down in college football history as one of the best trick plays ever."

Tom Mars kept that from happening.

The first time Tom and I connected, he assured me I had a strong case against Golf Channel. The only downside initially was that he doesn't accept any case on a contingency basis, and his services aren't cheap. It was a tough decision, but one I knew I had to make—even with my dwindling income and soon-to-be expiring benefits. Sarah and I talked it over, and we both quickly came to the same conclusion. We were willing to do whatever it took to ensure that Golf Channel didn't get away with what they'd done. We also wanted to send a clear message to prevent the network from ever committing similar wrongdoings to other employees ever again, especially women.

Once Tom and I agreed to work together, he was all in. We had many long conversations initially, and they weren't just limited to attorney/client information. I could tell that Tom cared—not only about my case, but about me as a person as well. It was reassuring to know I had the right lawyer representing me. But it also gave me an enormous sense of security because I felt as though I had a pseudo-brother on my side ready to go to battle in my defense.

For the next couple of weeks, I sent Tom everything—text messages and emails from Molly and Geoff over the years as well as similar documentation from other key contributors; detailed notes of the run-ins with Brandel that I began taking once I sensed there was an ongoing issue; plus notes from other employees who I knew had issues of mistreatment. After taking in all the information, talking to potential witnesses, and numerous follow-up calls with long lists of questions, Tom did what he does best. He put his head down and went to work.

CHAPTER 27

DEAR DAVID COHEN

THE FIRST MOVE Tom made once he'd had enough time to thoroughly research and consider everything involving my case was to reach out to David Cohen, Comcast's senior counselor and advisor and a longtime acquaintance of his. Tom was reasonably certain that Mr. Cohen would look at the evidence we'd compiled and handle my grievance in a timely manner. Since they'd worked together on other important cases in the past, Tom felt confident that David knew he wouldn't waste his time with far-fetched nonsense and disprovable claims.

Early on in his email to Cohen (dated March 5, 2020), Tom affirmed: "As you know, I'm at a point in my career where I'm extremely selective about what matters I'll take on and who I will represent. In fact, for that very reason, I no longer represent the client whose grievance you helped resolve the last time we talked. That said, I'm now representing a client of the highest character with an outstanding reputation, and her grievance with a Comcast affiliate is demonstrably meritorious."

Besides laying out my specific accusations, Tom also took time to build our argument that the network's misogynist culture could be traced back all the way to the early days at Golf Channel as well as recent transgressions at NBCUniversal.

He mentioned the Matt Lauer scandal and Ronan Farrow's book, which detailed how Ronan was censored (and eventually fired) by NBC senior producers for reporting on credible sexual harassment and assault claims against Lauer, Chris Matthews, and Harvey Weinstein. In the same section, he also included firsthand accounts from other women he'd interviewed during his discovery process.

These accounts included women confirming that Golf Channel had engaged in numerous sexist behaviors. Like my situation, Tom found that Mark Summer had mistreated other female employees while I was there, which included creepily harping on how employees dressed.

From the letter: "Among other things, [the employee] came forward with evidence that Summer repeatedly complained that [her] 'athletic, tanned legs' were distracting him 'and other people' at work, that her skirts were 'too tight and too short,' and that she should 'dress more like Hillary Clinton and wear pants to work. On one occasion, Summer made these inappropriate comments to [the accuser] during a meeting with Patti Lewis [director of HR for TGC since November 2014], who expressed no concern or objection to Summer's statements. During our investigation, other female employees of TGC expressed their opinion that there was nothing provocative or inappropriate about [her] attire and that Summer seemed to be infatuated with her. These employees remarked that Summer had likewise been obsessed with Angela Akins, another female employee who eventually left TGC to marry the celebrity pro golfer, Sergio Garcia."

Tom went on to note that Mark Summer had never given me a bad performance review and then highlighted the boys' club culture that covered for guys like Mark, recounting the "any trained monkey" incident specifically as proof that some high-profile men there were above the law.

The letter continued with in-depth descriptions of the various problems I'd faced throughout my years at Golf Channel. These included the previously mentioned on-air and office antics by Brandel, being outed as gay at work, being taken off and then reinstated on the CME tournament, the NCAA slight at Arkansas, plus the multiple witnesses who'd confirmed that there seemed to be a conspiracy by Chamblee and other influential people to push me out.

Tom also mentioned my contacting Susanna Zwerling in NBCUniversal's compliance department. He explained how she informed Golf Channel's HR department that I'd made a statement on record that led to an investigation after I'd begged her to keep it between us before disclosing anything, which she agreed to do. He finished the letter by telling Mr. Cohen that even though Golf Channel had reduced my contract to part-time based on their assertion that it was merely budget cuts, they "continued to spend money like a drunken sailor in late 2019. That didn't change in 2020, as illustrated by the decision to relocate TGC's headquarters. Furthermore, TGC renewed a number of other 'on-air' contracts for 2020, including a contract with [my] replacement—a white male in his early [fifties]."

As stated earlier, according to Tom (and as far as I was concerned), his letter should've done the trick. He told me to sit tight and that, hopefully, we'd get a constructive response sooner rather than later. When we did receive the response a few days later, it wasn't quite what Tom had expected. Mr. Cohen simply told him he couldn't get involved and was sending his letter to the NBCUniversal lawyers.

Undeterred, eight days later, we moved forward and filed our first charge of discrimination and retaliation with the EEOC.

CHAPTER 28

EEOC, PART I

THE FIRST OFFICIAL statement from NBCUniversal to the EEOC was signed by Temitope K. Yusuf, the network's vice president of employment. After a brief introduction, she got straight to work, quickly discrediting my charges. To paraphrase her opening remarks, Yusuf boldly stated that there was no merit to any of my claims and that Tom and I had strewn hyperbolic hot air throughout our submission. The most ironic part was that she literally employed her own hyperbole while hammering me for verbal puffery. I had to laugh reading their lawyer's use of flagrant metaphors while ringing me up for the absolute truth.

But Ms. Yusuf's rebuttal was far from finished. She briefly shifted gears from attacking my integrity and took the position that if Golf Channel was truly trying to retaliate against me, why would they have given me another three-year contract after some of the alleged incidents occurred? I suppose it was her job to ignore the fact that my relationship with Geoff went south long after the new contract was signed, which is when the bulk of the retaliatory acts began to take place.

Next, Ms. Yusuf alleged that throughout my time at Golf Channel, I'd been unable to make the difficult inquiries with my subjects that a reporter is expected to do. As her only example, she brought up the time when I interviewed LPGA superstar Lexi Thompson just minutes after she missed a two-foot putt to win the CME Group Tour Championship. Instead of asking Lexi about her failure while she was in tears, I decided to take a different approach with the interview. I mentioned her obvious disappointment right off the top and then transitioned to my question about her still winning the season-ending Race to the CME Globe and its $1 million bonus.

Even though I never received a single year-end performance review regarding my on-air work that was anything but positive overall, let's put a pin in the claim that I was bad at conducting interviews. In fact, it was the part of the job that I enjoyed the most and also where I received the most positive feedback. In the one and only example that Ms. Yusuf provided, the interview with Lexi Thompson in the 2017 CME Group Tour Championship, she couldn't have been more off the mark.

Lexi is, without question, the LPGA Tour's biggest star. When she's in or near the lead, the television ratings skyrocket. More importantly, she's also an incredibly nice person with a huge heart. No matter what Lexi shoots or how disappointed she is when a win slips away, she always stays afterward to sign autographs for her adoring fans, which sometimes includes smiling through the pain that the game of golf can unfortunately provide all too often. For these reasons and more, I've always had a soft spot for Lexi.

Even though she's an 11-time winner on tour and a major champion, she's faced more on-course heartache than any professional golfer I know. As a member of the media, I was always unbiased in my reporting. But I'm also sensitive to human beings and what they're going through, especially when it's on public display. When Lexi missed that two-foot putt, I could tell how much she was hurting.

Her mental health at that moment was a hell of a lot more important to me than asking a question I knew would only invoke more negative emotion and tears. That's not in my playbook as an interviewer.

According to Ms. Yusuf, when Mark Summer told me that I needed to bring up Lexi's failure, I insisted to him that I was right and became contentious when he pushed back on my point of view, which is entirely incorrect. As I stated in my portion of the EEOC response to NBCUniversal, "When Mark called me into his office after the CME event to talk about not asking her about the putt, I explained my reasons. He told me that I still have to ask the question, no matter. I told him I understood his point and would remember it in the future. That meeting never once got heated. We talked it over and quickly moved on."

Once again, the NBCUniversal lawyer was using inflammatory language to portray me as a weak interviewer who was terrible at taking feedback from my bosses, despite having numerous emails and texts proving that I not only listened to their feedback, but I welcomed and appreciated it as well.

Throughout Ms. Yusuf's response, she lasered in on the different times that I'd alleged gender, age, and sexual orientation discrimination. When my being outed as gay at work came up, she danced around the issue entirely. Instead, she painted Mark's actions as an honest mistake, motivated by a principled desire to make sure that I wasn't dating an LPGA pro in defiance of (unwritten) company policy. The situation with Angela Akins and Sergio Garcia was invoked as justification as to why Mark Summer was so meticulous with his investigation of my Facebook post with Sarah in Thailand. She dismissed it as a non-issue because Geoff Russell never told Mark I'd already disclosed our relationship to him as if Geoff's oversight was a fair mistake. Also, because I didn't disclose to Mark, Geoff, or HR at the time that I felt harassed and humiliated by Mark's spreading rumors around the office, it didn't qualify as any type of discrimination under company policy.

The short answer to all the above: wow.

The next allegation Ms. Yusuf tried to diffuse was my being snubbed for the NCAA Women's Golf Championship in Arkansas. Attempting to kill four birds with one stone, she simultaneously took on my retaliation, gender, age, and sexual discrimination charges.

The crux of her argument was that I hadn't been slighted when Golf Channel tapped George Savaricas to host the NCAA Women's and Men's Championships. According to NBCUniversal, the move to have George assume the role that I'd occupied for several years prior was a combination of the good job he did at the men's tournament and a desire to save money. They framed my being upset about it (due to the fact the women's event was being held in my hometown, where I played college golf) as overreactive and off-base. Since all of this was supposedly due to economic and better-fit reasons, Ms. Yusuf attested that none of it had anything to do with discrimination or retaliatory intent.

I find it bizarre that this lawyer pivoted back and forth between claiming I wasn't good at my job and then suddenly acting like moving me off the assignment was merely a budgetary move. Adding in the fact that I'd been the host for years prior, and it was in my hometown, and where I played college golf, the idea that this was purely due to budget and George's good work at the men's tournament was a reach at best. Besides, the budget theory doesn't fly because instead of bringing in an extra host, they ended up bringing in an extra reporter, so no money was saved by this move at all.

But the most mind-boggling argument was yet to come.

Ms. Yusuf took one run at the Brandel Chamblee psychodrama that kept brewing throughout my time at Golf Channel. First, she played up the fact that I wasn't a regular on the higher-profile weekend broadcasts that Brandel was typically a part of, stating that only on occasion was I asked to fill in for other hosts. Then she boldly claimed that I was consistently unable to do my job well in these positions. As her only example, she brought up the time I'd struggled to make sense of the graphic during the broadcast, where Brandel threw a fit and waved his arms wildly at me off-camera. The way she flipped it, I'd not only failed to analyze the information properly, but I'd also caused Brandel distress because he was unable to follow up with an appropriate response afterward. This made him reasonably angry because he took his job seriously. If it wasn't such a serious accusation, how ridiculously off the mark she was would've been laughable.

Ms. Yusuf went on to assert that when Mark Summer tried to talk with me about the blow-up, I became defensive and contentious. It laid all the blame for Brandel's boorishness at my feet because I was the one who'd made an unreasonable mistake as if he and everyone else hadn't ever once slipped up on live television before.

In his response, Tom challenged her rebukes perfectly:

> I've seen what I call this desperate defense a few times before, but it's pretty unusual. The Golf Channel's central defense of their position is that Brandel's an asshole to everybody. He was not any more of an asshole to Lisa than he was to a bunch of other people, men and women. That's kind of interesting, but it's also interesting that you also don't see a line of men anywhere complaining about how Brandel mistreated them.

It's very telling that Ms. Yusuf altogether avoided the reports that two credible sources had witnessed Brandel admitting he was the ringleader of a campaign to get me fired. Not surprisingly, they tiptoed around everything except the night I had trouble with the graphic and then justified why Brandel went ballistic. NBCUniversal framed his outburst as mere frustration. I can only imagine what would've happened had the tables been turned and I behaved similarly to him on live TV.

Later, Ms. Yusuf also argued that since Mark Summer and Brandel Chamblee weren't the people who directly demoted me, they didn't cause that to happen and therefore bore no responsibility for the alleged discrimination. That one still makes my head spin.

The rest of Ms. Yusuf's defense of NBCUniversal boiled down to the fact that I hadn't directly told my managers, HR, and compliance that I felt discriminated against due to my age, gender, and sexual orientation. Due to that technicality, none of what they did to me was legally provable on those grounds. Calling this response disingenuous doesn't cut it. It was equal parts flimsy and narcissistic. She literally seemed to be daring Tom and me to take our EEOC case the distance, knowing the emotional and financial hurdles might be difficult to overcome. However, as if it was a cruel gift from the gods, within weeks of NBCUniversal's implicit denial of my situation and just one week before our response to it was due, Geoff Russell put all his cards on the table during the 2019 ANA Inspiration.

CHAPTER 29

FRUIT BASKET

I'm not ready to make nice...I'm not ready to back down.
I'm still mad as hell, and I don't have time...
To go 'round and 'round and 'round.
It's too late to make it right...I probably wouldn't if I could.
'Cause I'm mad as hell...Can't bring myself to do what it is...
You think I should.

—The Chicks, "Not Ready to Make Nice"

INSTINCT IS AN INTERESTING PHENOMENON. It's hard to define and impossible to explain. Before Round One of the ANA Inspiration began, I spent that morning walking in circles around the hotel where we were staying at Mission Hills. I can't tell you how many laps I did or how many times I listened to "Not Ready to Make Nice" by The Chicks. It was almost as if fate was telling me I needed it. Three badass women who refused to back down or give in when country music attempted to sabotage their historical career. In 2003, the top-selling female group of all time was basically canceled by country radio and many country music fans after publicly opposing the War in Iraq and President George W. Bush specifically. This song was their response to all those who'd written them off and wanted them to "just shut up and sing."

When Chapter 1 ended, Mark Summer had just called me back with the shocking news: "Geoff wanted me to call you and tell you to come home."

As soon as I got back on the other line with Tom after speaking to Mark, I'm not sure who was more shocked, him or me. Just think about this fiasco: a woman, who was covering a women's major championship in the middle of an EEOC case alleging gender discrimination and retaliation, was being sent home by a 60-something-year-old white man over a gender-related issue one week before our final response to the EEOC was due.

It's a lot to take in, I know.

Tom being Tom—clever and to the point—jokingly asked, "Where do I send Geoff a fruit basket?" We both laughed. I definitely needed it more at that moment than he did.

As soon as the final putt dropped on that Sunday of the ANA Inspiration, the *Golf Central* Twitter account posted a "correction" to my reporting. I was at home watching the coverage and couldn't believe my eyes when I saw it. It was loaded with errors and half-truths. Paris (the club-fitter) called me. He was furious. Janet (the player) texted Sarah and me both about it, in disbelief. I spoke with Tony (the swing coach), and he was close to losing it because of how twisted and off-base it was. None of us could believe that a national network dared to post something so mindfully misguided on social media in an attempt to cover up its wrongdoings. Here is the statement, inflammatorily written by Geoff Russell, which is amazingly still available online as of the writing of this book:

A correction.

Golf Channel has done additional reporting on the story involving LPGA player Xiyu Lin and the new set of irons she debuted at the ANA Inspiration. Here is what we found out.

Lin spent the week before the ANA working with Paris Fisher, a clubfitter at Orlando's Golf Fitting Studios, who recommended she try a new set of irons consisting of Mizuno clubheads and Nippon Neo shafts.

Since Xiyu is not a Mizuno staff player (Mizuno has no staff players on the LPGA Tour), Fisher called Mizuno's Jeff Cook, who lives in Indianapolis and runs the company's tour program, and asked if a set with those components could be built and delivered to Xiyu quickly (Mizuno said the request was one day; Fisher said it was 2–3 days).

According to a Mizuno spokesperson, because the company's tour equipment reps typically require a player's current set of clubs to use as a baseline when building a new set, because there was confusion over the exact specs of the new set, and because Mizuno didn't have the Nippon Neo shafts Xiyu requested, Cook told Fisher he couldn't provide the clubs within the accelerated timeframe.

So Fisher and Xiyu tried other sources. They purchased a set of Mizuno irons from an Edwin Watts store in Orlando—which Xiyu paid for. Fisher contacted Nippon, which sent him the shafts. Fisher then replaced the existing shafts in the irons he purchased with the Nippons, and Xiyu had her clubs in time to travel to California for the ANA.

Mizuno's spokesperson told Golf Channel, "Our only connection to this story is that the clubheads in Xiyu's new irons are Mizunos." Our initial reporting on this story left the impression that Mizuno made Xiyu pay for the clubs, when that was not the case. Golf Channel regrets the error.

Two days later, Mizuno posted its own denial of my reporting on Twitter, too, which completely avoided any wrongdoing on the company's part. This, despite a conversation I had with two executives from Mizuno—both of whom said they would talk to the tour rep and put out a statement supporting Janet, Paris, and the LPGA Tour and acknowledge any mistake that anyone in their company made. Of course, none of that ended up happening, and instead, they chose to twist the story to avoid any culpability.

Correction to LPGA story recently escalated on social media

The report that Mizuno requested payment from an LPGA player to provide a set of irons in the build up to the ANA Inspiration tournament is inaccurate. Mizuno's tour team made a judgement [sic] that the request was made too close to the start of the tournament. The player then purchased irons locally. Mizuno did not request or receive payment from the player to provide product.

Mizuno proudly supports many players around the world, both male and female—paid and unpaid. Last weekend on the Ladies European Tour, the winner used Mizuno irons, having been supported unofficially for several years. There are also instances of both male and female players purchasing Mizuno equipment at golf shops (without our knowledge) for use at tour events.

Even though Golf Channel and Mizuno went to great lengths to discredit me, they were still exposed for their false claims by two very credible sources—Janet and Paris, both of whom called them out for their dishonesty online. This was Janet's response to Mizuno, which she quote tweeted:

> Hi @MizunogolfNA I'm the player in this statement N this & the @golfcentral statement is inaccurate. I was in the room when @ParisFisherPGA made the call to the tour rep on 8/31. It was "sorry no" so I went and bought the clubs locally. This is 10 days (before) the tournament started

And this is what Paris Fisher posted in response to Golf Channel's "correction" statement, which was also quote tweeted:

> This correction needs a correction @GolfChannel & @MizunoGolfNA. I am the fitter mentioned in this statement and it has many inaccuracies. We wanted heads so i [sic] could build them & they said there was nothing they could do. Unfortunately a common occurrence for @LPGA players

As you can imagine, their tweets blew up. The social media backlash to all of this was enormous. Golf Channel and Mizuno were absolutely hammered in the comment threads of their ridiculous "correction" tweets. Most reasonable people could smell that something was fishy with the undertone of their words. What started as a flimsy attempt to poke holes in my journalistic integrity had metastasized into a full-fledged fiasco for both companies. To this day, neither organization has publicly admitted any wrongdoing—nor have they offered an apology to Janet, Paris, or me for their recklessly inaccurate "correction" statements.

With all of this taking place, Tom had to ask for a delay with our final EEOC response because there were several new chapters he needed to add to this already unfortunate story. Still, as bad as it

was then, it'd soon get even worse. Per Tom's request, I immediately
emailed the head of human resources at Golf Channel, Julie Lusk, to
get everything that had just happened documented. It wouldn't take
long before I realized just how skilled Golf Channel is in the cover-up
and denial department.

After six days of asking questions and failing to get any sort of
answers (or anything close to an apology), I sent Lusk another email—
this time with some demands:

September 17, 2020

Julie

Since you have made a request of me to not post anything on
Twitter involving the Mizuno incident, I have a few requests
and questions for you—some that I've been trying to get
answered since last Friday.

As you know and as we've discussed, I was sent home
that Friday (Sept. 11th) by Geoff Russell and immediately
filed an HR complaint with you based on his use of profanity and screaming at me over a tweet I made the day prior.
One hour later I was sent home for no reason.

I requested an explanation from you as to why I was
sent home in our first conversation on Monday (Sept. 14)
and again yesterday (Sept. 16). But you still haven't provided
me with an official reason as to why I was sent home—this
despite telling me the investigation and case against Geoff
Russell has been "closed" and action has been taken. I'm
assuming the action you told me that has been taken against
Geoff as a result of your investigation did not involve any
type of suspension since I saw him (from a distance) at Golf
Channel late yesterday afternoon?

If the case is "closed," can you please tell me when I will receive notice explaining why I was sent home? And if there is no valid reason, will Golf Channel or Geoff apologize publicly for the error?

Speaking of apologies, I notified you in my HR complaint against Geoff how he verbally berated me and repeatedly used profanity during that abusive outburst. I expect a written apology from him for that behavior. Again, since the case is "closed" hopefully you understand that an apology is warranted. Will you, or anyone associated with Golf Channel/NBC, be asking him to provide that apology?

Can you also please provide me with, as I requested on Monday as well, the Golf Channel/NBC policy regarding an upper level employee (like Geoff Russell, SVP) who verbally berates and uses profanity with a lower-level employee like me (freelance reporter)?

Can you please provide me with a time frame as to when this new investigation you mentioned yesterday will be closed? Because of the inaccurate "correction" tweet that Golf Channel posted on Twitter (via the Golf Central account with over 95,000 followers), people on Twitter are now questioning my journalistic integrity.

I will never understand why Golf Channel rushed to put out this inaccurate "correction" (one that both the player and club fitter have responded to claiming its inaccuracies) in defense of Mizuno so quickly—and without properly notifying me or even talking to me about it. The last communication I've had with anyone from Golf Channel involving this matter was when Geoff screamed and used abusive language six days ago.

Lastly, if Geoff was just attempting to get the facts straight, why did he leave out the most important part of the conversation he had with Paris Fisher (Xiyu Lin's club fitter/builder) regarding Mizuno denying to send her six iron heads...and after that Mizuno rejecting Xiyu's offer to purchase the tour heads from Mizuno?

Geoff leaving those key facts out of the "correction" statement on Twitter shows his only desire was to prove my tweet and on-air statement to be factually incorrect in his attempt to justify his irrational behavior (which is never justifiable, no matter).

It is the clear definition of a WITCH HUNT by a bully who was abusing his power.

My attorneys and I not only expect, but demand, a swift resolution to your new investigation as well as a written apology from Geoff and a tweet from Golf Channel clearing up this blatant error by the Network that has done harm to my professional reputation.

Regards,

Lisa

My back-and-forth email exchange with her was clearly a bust. There was no remorse on Golf Channel's part whatsoever, and the "apology" we had to demand from Geoff, which I received the following day, was about as cold and disingenuous as they get.

September 18, 2020

Lisa,

I'm writing to follow up on our call last week to apologize for my tone and manner. Rest assured it will not happen again.

Regards,

Geoff

Notice the last sentence of Geoff's forced email to me: *Rest assured it will not happen again.* It was a camouflaged threat, masquerading as contrition. Since he didn't adequately define what it was that wouldn't happen again, let me provide some clarity.

From that day forward, I never interviewed another LPGA player during a live broadcast—not at the KPMG Women's PGA Championship the following month; not at the U.S. Women's Open; and not at the CME Group Tour Championship in December, where I'd always interviewed players for the live tournament broadcasts. Instead, Golf Channel flew in three different people to do those jobs in my place… all during a so-called "budget crisis."

Geoff was right. It wouldn't happen again because he further diminished my role. What astounds me most about the entire situation is that, again, Golf Channel wasn't even doing business with Mizuno when this happened. Only recently, after I was long gone, has Mizuno started buying ad time on-air. Back then, they were just helping each other swat a pesky fly that had gotten in the ointment.

As for the explanation as to why I was sent home, here's a portion of the email Julie Lusk sent me on September 21, 2020, which never specifically addressed the issue:

> When asked about whether you reached out to Mizuno prior to publishing the tweet, you stated that you had not contacted them to understand their position. You also stated that you did not see your tweet as a story but instead as your opinion.
>
> …You should have clearly indicated that you were stating your opinion and should have discussed the tweet with your manager before posting since you were citing your opinion involving a golf equipment company.
>
> Our investigation determined that your story was incomplete as was the correction tweeted by Golf Central.

She used the word "opinion" seven times in that email. I never once said what happened with Janet's irons was my opinion. What I tweeted and said in the interview were facts that Janet, Paris, and Tony all publicly confirmed. Julie Lusk hung onto the word "opinion" because that's all she had. It didn't hold water then and still doesn't now. As for talking to Mizuno, I did that, too, and the company has never given me a reason why they wouldn't give Janet the irons.

My main resolution from the "Mizuno Incident" was a steadfast commitment to expose the Geoff Russells and Julie Lusks of the world. That commitment began as soon as I landed in Orlando and watched the last two rounds of the ANA Inspiration…on my sofa.

CHAPTER 30

EEOC, PART II

_____

IT'S STILL HARD to fully comprehend the recklessness of the ANA Inspiration fiasco. Most notably, how it happened on the heels of NBCUniversal denying any responsibility for Golf Channel's retaliatory behavior and less than one week before our response to Temitope Yusuf's challenges was due. Because of this, Tom and I were loaded for bear when we sent our strongly worded response to NBCUniversal's letter.

Tom, as he often likes to do, led off with loud shots fired:

> Before I address the glaring misstatements and omissions in TGC's Position Statement, I wish to thank TGC Senior Vice President and Executive Editor Geoff Russell for digging an even deeper hole for TGC to climb out of in connection with this charge of discrimination and retaliation. As explained below, Executive Editor Russell's recent mistreatment of Ms. Cornwell provided an excellent, but troubling, illustration of TGC's blatantly retaliatory intentions and discriminatory employment practices.

As evidenced by the documents set forth in the Appendix to the letter, on Thursday, September 10, 2020, while covering an LPGA golf tournament in Southern California, Ms. Cornwell posted a comment on Twitter calling out Mizuno, a golf equipment supplier, for its unequal treatment of LPGA golfers. The next day, Executive Editor Russell called Ms. Cornwell and immediately started berating her for mentioning on Twitter that Mizuno had double standards in its dealing with male and female pro golfers. The minute that Ms. Cornwell started to explain to Executive Editor Russell why her Twitter post was both appropriate and accurate, he unleashed a profane tirade so loud that it could have been heard by others and repeatedly screamed: 'I don't give a shit what you think!' At that point, Ms. Cornwell told Executive Editor Russell that she would not tolerate that kind of verbal abuse and ended the call.

A short while later, a TGC senior officer called Ms. Cornwell to tell her that Executive Editor Russell had instructed him to inform her that she was being taken off the air immediately and should fly back to her home in Florida. Ms. Cornwell asked for an explanation of this decision, but none was provided. She emailed a complaint to the head of TGC's HR department later that evening describing in detail exactly what happened. As instructed by Executive Editor Russell, Ms. Cornwell flew back to Florida the next day.

Next, we detailed how the day after I left, Golf Channel posted a correction tweet, asserting that I'd misreported that Mizuno had snubbed an LPGA player, which I'd verified with Xiyu Lin and her clubfitter Paris Fisher. Tom included the corrections to Golf Channel's correction statement by both witnesses and noted the "firestorm of media criticism" that the network's tweet received throughout the comment threads. It was also essential to highlight the fact that Geoff Russell apologized (albeit not on his own, but rather one that I had to demand) to me by email for his profanity-laced tongue-lashing.

This became one of the main themes of our response. NBCUniversal's defensive counterclaims were misleading, and the discrimination and retaliation allegations they dismissed were still ongoing. If anything, it seemed like our EEOC filing had triggered Geoff, and he was going out of his way to make things worse. To use some more hyperbole here, they were making it a game of emotional chicken.

Tom continued throughout the reply to hammer NBCUniversal's lawyers for portraying me as an underachieving employee. He pointed out that all of my attached performance reviews (completed by Mark Summer) had been predominantly positive, with only a few minor criticisms.

> The only criticisms in her only two annual reviews are the subjective opinions of Ms. Cornwell's immediate supervisor, Mark Summer—the TGC officer who would later lead the campaign to get rid of Ms. Cornwell. In Summer's evaluation of Ms. Cornwell's performance, he commented that Ms. Cornwell needed to display a "higher level of enthusiasm and consistency" and "increase energy level"—whatever that means. The other comments by Summer were either accolades or suggestions to "work on" this or that ("Continue to work on being an even better interviewer").
>
> As the EEOC knows, such vague comments made about female television personalities are, more often than not, the product of subconscious gender bias. If the female journalist doesn't fit their male supervisor's preconceived notion of how women should present themselves, they may end up being labeled "not strong or energetic enough." On the other end of the spectrum, if they have the strength and

enthusiasm to express their own views with confidence, they may end up being labeled a "bitch." TGC's Position Statement attempts to attach both derogatory labels to Ms. Cornwell at the same time yet fails to mention that her performance reviews paint a very different picture.

The other piece of the performance reports that had to be addressed was the fact that, for some unexplained reason, Mark Summer never gave me one in my final year. Not only is this type of oversight extremely unusual, but it also again looked to us like another way for Golf Channel to give themselves wiggle room when they let me go for no better reason. Most importantly for NBCUniversal's lawyers, it gave them plausible deniability of their baseless accusations that I'd been bad at my job. Six years of excellent feedback be damned; for all their legal team knew, Mark, Geoff, and Molly could've been referring to the present.

A major point that needed refuting from our first round of submissions was the defense's declaration that the other women's stories we detailed, claiming harassment by Mark Summer, were "irrelevant." While they weren't directly involved with my experiences, their run-ins with Mark Summer and other threatening managers helped us establish a pattern of misogyny, retaliation, and sexual discrimination at Golf Channel. Especially considering NBC's problems with Matt Lauer and Chris Matthews, the whole network had an apparent track record of enabling high-ranking men to get away with mistreating female subordinates.

Tom used previously established legal precedent to debunk the idea that just because Mark Summer and Brandel Chamblee didn't demote me, it didn't mean their behavior wasn't responsible for it.

Perhaps TGC ignored this evidence because it asserts that Mark Summer and Brandel Chamblee played no role in the decision to demote Ms. Cornwell. So what? The United States Supreme Court has made clear that the actions of an employee's supervisor, acting with discriminatory intent, that poison the opinion of the ultimate decision maker, can establish the proximate cause required to bring an action for unlawful employment practices.

In a precedent-setting case known as *Staub v. Proctor Hospital* it was legally established that "if a supervisor performs an act motivated by antimilitary animus that is intended by the supervisor to cause an adverse employment action, and if that act is a proximate cause of the ultimate employment action, then the employer is liable."

To sum it up in straightforward terms, NBCUniversal claimed that they didn't retaliate against me because I was demoted purely for budgetary reasons. However, my HR complaint was filed only nine months before Molly told my agent I was being demoted—a timeframe that would've raised a red flag with almost anyone. Regardless, they asserted that since this blow to my livelihood didn't happen simultaneously with my complaint, it couldn't be considered retaliation. So basically, they waited for a convenient time to try to avoid any appearance that they were retaliating against me. If anything, it makes it sneaky as well as petty.

After Tom's comments, I had the opportunity to speak for myself in our response as well. Early on, I affirmed:

Let me just say that I'm very proud of the work I've done for TGC since the start of my employment in 2014. It certainly hasn't been perfect. But I sleep well at night knowing that I represented (and continue to represent) the Network very well with hard work, dedication, and an extensive knowledge of the game.

Then I shared a screenshot of an email from Molly, where she lauded me for my pre-coverage at the same NCAA Women's Championship that the NBCUniversal lawyer mentioned in her denial. *Lisa, so much terrific coverage of you and the Arkansas program. Great job representing us.*

I explained why the week of the NCAAs was so disappointing and took issue with NBCUniversal's flip-flopping between saying I was merely being cut to part-time because of budgetary reasons and then accusing me of being underwhelming and unprofessional at my job. I shared numerous text messages from Mark Summer where he praised me for doing, in his words, "Good work!" More importantly, I once again laid out the timeline of events that led me to the harsh realization that retaliation was indeed in play.

A big sticking point with NBCUniversal's defense was that they claimed, "Unbeknownst to Mr. Summer, Ms. Cornwell had informed Mr. Russell of her relationship, but asked him not to disclose it to anyone."

Quoting myself again:

> This is incorrect for two reasons. First of all, Molly and Geoff told me that they weren't going to mention this to anyone (including Mark and Adam) and that it was up to me if I wanted to disclose it to them, which I chose not to do because, to be honest, I didn't trust them. Secondly, Mark and Adam were already aware that I'd revealed my relationship to Molly and Geoff when our meeting began because the first thing they said to me was, "We know you told Molly and Geoff about your relationship with Sarah, but we don't think you were honest about her LPGA status with them."

It was glaringly obvious when I described how Sarah's LPGA status actually worked to Mark and Adam that they had no idea what they were talking about. It also became clear that Molly and Geoff had already signed off on removing me from CME before realizing I was right in my rebuttal. As soon as I set the record straight, Geoff started squirming. The minute Mark and Adam left the room, he apologized to me, saying he had no idea that the other men were going to "ambush" me that way. One week later, Molly text messaged me and said I was back on the schedule for CME.

Coincidentally, Mark and Adam had a well-known close friendship for many years. Soon after that meeting with Geoff, Adam was fired. That is yet another reason Mark would have clear motivation to retaliate against me.

My reply to the EEOC once again covered many more significant events in this book. These included my demotion at the NCAA Women's Championship, the sordid history with Brandel Chamblee, and my attempts to mend the fence with him along the way. Brandel's campaign to get me fired was outlined in detail, including his admission to it.

Still, the other women who'd shared their stories of mistreatment and lent their names to the cause seemed most important to focus on. All combined, 10 other women signed off on us including them in our submission to the EEOC. Every one of them has my utmost respect and gratitude. Sadly, due to various reasons mentioned before, including NDAs and retaliation concerns of their own, most of these women wish to remain anonymous. I understand how complicated it is to put your reputation and livelihood on the line by going public with your experiences. Again, I'm just thankful they were willing to contribute to our case. There is most assuredly power in numbers.

After I wrapped up my narrative, Tom's final summation couldn't have been better:

Despite Russell's use of the word "apology" in his recent e-mail to Ms. Cornwell, neither he nor his executive

colleagues are sorry for what they've done to Ms. Cornwell. They're not sorry for trying to run her off. They're
not sorry for demoting her. They're not sorry for smearing
her reputation as an accomplished journalist on the world's
largest social media platform. If they were sorry about anything they've done to Ms. Cornwell or their other female
employees over the years, they would have done something
by now to change TGC's culture and hold their executives
accountable for their misconduct.

The only thing TGC's executives are sorry about is that
they didn't realize their latest victim of discrimination and
retaliation had the courage, stamina, and resources to do
something about it. That said, Ms. Cornwell can't change
the employment practices of TGC on her own. Without
intervention by the EEOC, TGC will continue to operate
as just another NBC affiliate that doesn't "give a shit" about
equality in the workplace.

For the second time, we thought this strongly worded rebuttal
would compel NBCUniversal and Golf Channel to back off their vig-
orous defense and figure out a way to settle things. But, stuck in a
repeating loop, they were far from finished fanning the flames.

———————

Our next submission to the EEOC came the week that Golf Channel
tweeted out the press release announcing everyone who'd be covering the KPMG Women's PGA Championship for the network. This
was the next women's major on the schedule after Geoff cussed me
out and sent me home from the ANA Inspiration one month prior.
Even though I'd been on the schedule to work KPMG for months,
when I saw that Golf Channel had tweeted the release announcing

its on-air talent team for the event, my name was nowhere to be seen.

Being fully aware that this wasn't just a simple oversight, I emailed the release to Julie Lusk in HR and asked, "Notice anything in this press release?"

Her response: "That you aren't included? If so, I checked in with Communication/PR and this came from their office with no input from others."

What a convenient coincidence.

Later that month, after pressing Julie about my contract renewal for more than a week, she finally informed me that she'd spoken with Molly and that Golf Channel wouldn't be able to renew my contract because of continued downsizing within the network. I already knew that answer, but I just needed her to make it official so Tom could start planning his next move.

Tom relayed this information to my EEOC case investigator, maintaining that it was "a calculated gender-based, retaliatory strategy intended to expel Ms. Cornwell from the TGC boys club."

Meanwhile, the countdown to the end of my time at Golf Channel was now ticking. I only had two more events to work. Finally, on December 20, 2020, I posted the following tweet on my final day to officially say goodbye:

> Hard to believe today's my last final rd. w/Golf Channel.
> Of all my roles, nothing's meant more than covering the
> @LPGA. For a girl who grew up dreaming of doing what
> they do, it's been an honor.
> Thanks to everyone out here for your trust & friendship.
> Until next time, #DriveOn

The response to it was overwhelming. I'll forever be thankful to the 200-plus players, caddies, and fans of the game who responded with condolences, kindness, and appreciation to that tweet. It was an emotional day. I broke down with my field producer and photographer after we did our final live shot. Lexi Thompson's sweet mom, Judy, shed tears with me on the 18th tee box when she heard the news. It was a hard but special day and one that I'll never forget. As easy as it's been to look back on everything that went wrong during those seven years, what lives with me now, more than anything, is all that went right and the friendships I made. Those people made it worth it…every bit of it.

PART VI

REPERCUSSIONS

———

CHAPTER 31

JANUARY 2021

ALL THE SENTIMENTAL EMOTIONS I felt working my last event for Golf Channel would soon be replaced by an overwhelming amount of determination. I was home in Arkansas for the Christmas holiday and mentally preparing for what was next. I told Tom that even though we were still embroiled in the EEOC case, there was no way I was going to stay silent any longer. Less than a week before my contract officially ended on December 31, 2020, we began formulating a plan to make the loudest public statement possible as soon as I was free to do so.

Fortunately for me, Tom has this perfect mix of John Wayne's grittiness and Albert Einstein's genius. He and I spent the week after Christmas crafting a bulletproof statement, going back and forth to make sure it was just right. He deserves significant credit for formulating the well-aimed dagger I tweeted on New Year's Day.

Jan. 1, 2021
The first day in 7 years I'm not in a contract w/Golf Channel
& am free to speak up for the many women who've been

marginalized, belittled, berated & treated like second class citizens—including me.

The days of it being swept under the rug are over. #MoreToCome

What happened next was a huge surprise. Since being attacked is almost guaranteed when posting anything controversial on social media, the response was shockingly and overwhelmingly positive. That January 1 tweet now has thousands of likes and hundreds of comments and retweets with very few negative replies. The positive-to-negative comment ratio it received is almost unheard of. Just about everyone was encouraging and supportive, which meant a lot considering how angry and hurt I still was. It was the first sign in a long time that other people genuinely cared about this problem as much as I did. It also told me how much they respected my work, which meant more than I could ever express.

Another mind-blowing plot twist happened right after my tweet went viral. I went to Instagram, where I rarely engage with anyone, and posted a screenshot of my tweet. It didn't take long before my direct messages were filled with chat requests from women who'd read the tweet and wanted to share their own stories of mistreatment and abuse at Golf Channel and NBC Sports.

Before fully realizing the butterfly effect that had been set in motion, I was stunned to see so many others had suffered similar sexist and retaliatory slights at the hands of the same perpetrators. While their shocking testimonies were difficult to read and process, it was becoming clear that this wasn't just *my* problem and that I'd somewhat obliviously emboldened a wave of women to have their voices be heard, too—finally.

The stories they shared with me dealt with unjust behavior similar to what I'd endured from Mark Summer, Matt Ginella, Geoff Russell, Brandel Chamblee, Julie Lusk, and Molly Solomon. There were also stories involving sexual harassment, stalking, xenophobic/hate speech rhetoric, and, sadly, even worse. It was horrifying to read.

What made it more difficult to process was that most of the women I spoke with were bound and gagged by nondisclosure agreements resulting from private financial settlements with Golf Channel/NBCUniversal. Even some who weren't under NDAs feared of being blacklisted if they blew the whistle. The legitimate grief this caused them made us all go from rage to anguish, depression to despair, until apathy itself became our new opponent.

Soon after my tweet ignited Golf Twitter, I noticed that major news outlets were also paying attention. Besides the near-deluge of Instagram messages from spurned former female employees at Golf Channel and NBC Sports, I was also contacted by a producer from *CBS This Morning with Gayle King*. Tom and I had a conversation with her about my story, and then we didn't hear another word from CBS.

While disappointing, none of this was a surprise to us. Tom was quick to remind me that former CBS top dog, Les Moonves, was simultaneously defending sexual assault and discrimination allegations of his own. Zeroing in on a systemic problem they were enabling wouldn't be a smart move at that point for them. Like many other networks with closets full of skeletons, it was too risky to try and promote my cause while tiptoeing around all the others.

There were a few other prominent publications that reached out as well. We were approached by the *New York Times* and the *Atlantic*, among others. But, again, nothing ever came of our chats. However, shortly after those talks, I received an Instagram message from Chris Solomon, co-founder of *No Laying Up*, a popular online source for golf fans worldwide, inviting me to join him on their podcast to discuss my tweet and my story. I respected how Chris approached me and felt confident he'd give me a fair shake. Thankfully, my instincts were correct.

My only request to Chris was for Tom to appear on the podcast with me. It wasn't because we were worried that he or the *No Laying Up* crew would ambush me. It was actually quite the opposite. Tom knew how fresh my wounds were and my tendency to go from fired up to enraged when revisiting those raw emotions. His job was to ensure that I kept things to a controlled burn on air. The last thing we needed was to accidentally spark a huge wildfire and damage our EEOC case.

Chris did a fantastic job of asking difficult but insightful questions. More importantly, he did what skilled interviewers always do: he listened. When we finished, Tom and I were encouraged by the entire experience. After the podcast was released, I was overwhelmed by the outpouring of support from the listeners. I owe Chris Solomon and the *No Laying Up* team a debt of gratitude. Their willingness to have me on, risking potential access to other Golf Channel and NBCUniversal entities, speaks volumes of their character and authenticity.

For the first time since my January 1 tweet took off, it felt like the wind was finally at my back instead of blowing in my face. Within hours of the *No Laying Up* interview being released, even more messages from women I didn't know kept pouring into my inbox. It was touching to see so many people connecting with my story.

Jan. 11, 2021:

Just listened to your *No Laying Up* interview and had to reach out. I started at GC in 2015 and I have to thank you for speaking out about the marginalization of women at that company. I was passed over for multiple opportunities including a social media position for Golf Central where they straight up told me it was a "tough" environment so they went with a man who was actually fired not long after for tweeting a personal tweet from the Central account. It was such a toxic environment and I would talk to other women about how we would cry everyday on the way home because of the consistent disrespect and lack of support. Mark Summer was maybe the worst person I've ever worked with and I don't know if you knew Holly Antony but she was fantastic but never promoted or offered a raise under a male manager. She was consistently pushed aside for using her voice. Thank you for speaking out and using your voice to amplify this important issue which I know first hand affect[s] so many women.

It wasn't just women who reached out either. I received many supportive messages from my former male colleagues who also wanted to show their support.

Jan. 4, 2021:

Hey Lisa. Just listened to your podcast interview. We worked together for many years at GC although not directly. I was in charge of all post production that included editing and post audio. All of my interactions with you or you with my team were always very positive. You always said hello and were pleasant to me. My last day after 11 years at GC was 12/31 also. I will miss having my job and the things I built, but not the toxic environment that you and others endured. I'm a fan and support you and hope your fight comes out on the positive side of this. Best of luck and know that you're not alone.

Soon after the podcast was released, I got a follow on Twitter from a journalist named Ben Strauss. Within hours, he reached out via direct message, and a few days later, Tom and I agreed to do the story.

CHAPTER 32

WASHINGTON POST

AFTER A QUICK GOOGLE SEARCH, I learned that Ben Strauss is a reporter for the *Washington Post* who specifically covers sports and media. Even though I'd never heard of Ben before, I was well aware of the credible and authentic way the *Post* went about telling stories. Not long after I released my tweet on January 1, it somehow made its way to his feed because of the traction it generated on the social media platform. As he followed the story, he caught wind of the podcast that Tom and I did and started investigating my claims. "My part of the story is pretty similar to some of the other folks I wrote about," Ben confirmed. "The thing that started it was Lisa Cornwell going on the *No Laying Up* podcast."

After the podcast, I continued to have more women and many sympathetic men reach out to me with their own accounts of terrible mistreatment at Golf Channel and NBC Sports. They thanked me for bravely speaking out about the boys' club culture at both places and the retaliatory way that powerful men treated them and their loved ones. Some of their stories were scandalous, while others were all too familiar.

According to Ben, after he spoke with Tom and me, his investigation led him to 18 other women who added their voices and stories to his piece. The women he spoke with included those who disclosed stories similar to mine and some who shared encounters of aggressive sexual harassment. From Ben's *Washington Post* article: "In late 2012, a 22-year-old freelance production assistant received sexually explicit emails from her superior. According to emails reviewed by *The Post*, the supervisor wrote, 'I'd like to make love to you, and I dream about you every morning. Do you feel any connection to me in that way? If not, no big deal. We'll have the same work relationship we've had. The last thing I want to do is creep you out.'"

One year later, when the same woman reported more troubling behavior from the same manager, she finally submitted a complaint to human resources. When asked why she hadn't come forward before, she said it was due to fear of retaliation from the powerful men at the top. After she spoke with HR, she also sent this follow-up statement addressing how the network seemed to dismiss her complaints. "I want to have faith that Golf Channel is supporting me, the victim, on this issue, but that is not how I have been made to feel at the moment," she wrote, "I felt more like I was the one on trial."

This wasn't the only shocking incident Ben discovered. Others included a newly hired woman, on her first day no less, logging on to her new computer, and the first thing that popped up on her screen was a pornographic image of a naked woman. In 2009 there were reports of a "cock wall" where a group of men printed and posted emails and articles that included the word *cock* for public display at the office. It was considered lighthearted humor by those in power. As Ben would expose, this was the longstanding culture at Golf Channel.

These incidents didn't just occur before my 2014 arrival either. Besides sexism, they also included claims of racism. Again, from Ben's piece, "In 2019, a different woman was in the control room during an LPGA tournament, where a group of men were having a conversation about several Asian golfers. They described the women as having porcelain skin and looking like Japanese sex dolls, according to the woman and another who was told about the incident."

———————

One of the brave women who put her name in *The Post* was Chelsea Kite, a friend and former co-worker who was part of the live production team at Golf Channel from 2007 to 2019. During her interviews, Chelsea said that "a technical manager for live tournaments told her that he couldn't speak to her directly about her job performance because, as he put it, 'Women and people of color rule the world. We live in an HR world.'"

After Chelsea reported the manager, he was fired. However, it didn't take long before she was also let go for what Golf Channel told her was "a lack of commitment to her job despite positive performance reviews." Sound familiar? By the time Ben published his story, he'd become aware of several work-related lawsuits against Golf Channel that looked more like a trend than random occurrences. Many of these suits were still ongoing when I was hired.

Another woman who stuck her neck out was Jen Johnson. Again, from the *Washington Post* article: "The network's male-driven culture stunted some women's careers in broadcasting, former employees said. Jen Johnson, who worked in production from 2011 until last year, said she earned less than male colleagues and was asked by a higher-up whether having kids would negatively affect her career at Golf Channel."

Jen deserves a lot of credit for having my back over the past few years, and I'll always be grateful for the moral support she's given me every step of the way.

"She's fighting the good fight," said Johnson, "I'm thankful she's brought this as far as she has."

Jen wasn't the only woman who management targeted for having children. Back to Chelsea Kite, who learned the hard way that leadership seemed to paint motherhood and the desire to be a working mom as if it were some sort of disability. Families are something to be celebrated, not discouraged, especially in an industry like golf entertainment that brands itself as family oriented. Also, like it even needs to be said, but threatening women not to have kids (or else they won't move up in the company) comes awfully close to playing God.

Chelsea's story is similar to mine and so many other women in a multitude of ways, and given her bravery and willingness to speak out, I asked her to share some of what she encountered in her own words:

> Between 2011 and 2016, I had three beautiful children. During that time, I realized just how difficult it was to be a working mom employed by Golf Channel. I was scheduled to work two significant events for the network: The Open Championship at Royal Troon followed by the Rio Olympics. These were bucket-list moments for me, and I was on cloud nine in anticipation of the assignments. Even though the due date for my third child was just two weeks before the start of The Open, I decided to go back to work soon after giving birth because I didn't want to miss these once-in-a-lifetime opportunities. While it was a hard decision, I was fortunate to have excellent family support at home, which made it possible.
>
> Late in the pregnancy, my boss called to ask whether I would still be up for working so soon after having the baby. I told him absolutely. We had a plan in place, and I couldn't be more excited to go. Working these two events were going to be the highlights of my career, and they were too important to pass up. I might as well have said nothing because his response couldn't have been colder or more disingenuous:

"Chelsea, I just don't feel comfortable with you going, so I'm sorry, but I'm going to send someone else."

How did he have the right to make this decision for me? It was my body, my family, my choice. Plenty of mothers go back to work soon after giving birth. But this man, my boss, was dead set against it. So I missed out on The Open Championship—an opportunity of a lifetime—because a man thought he knew what was better for me as a mom. Besides the apparent condescension, it was textbook sexist behavior, too.

Everything inside me wanted to fight for what had become the biggest letdown of my professional career and something that I also knew was borderline illegal. I may not be a lawyer, but I know my fundamental rights as a human and employee. I debated whether to take this to our executive producer, Molly Solomon, since we had a good relationship at the time. Surely, as a mom to triplets, she would understand.

But I also worried that pushing back too hard would only make things worse, and I couldn't shake the feeling that this was some sort of delayed retaliation for reporting my boss' friend for a drunken outburst and unacceptable behavior on a work assignment (a couple of years prior) and him being forced to fire him afterward. In the back of my mind, I wondered if he was daring me to challenge him. That way, he could paint me as a problematic employee. These were the battles I was having in my head, even though my heart kept telling me to do something about it. In the end, fear won out, and I decided not to stir the pot.

The strong resentment I felt eventually faded but never entirely went away. I did my best to avoid exhibiting outward hostility toward my boss, but it was hard to be around him afterward. Almost two years later, the dynamic between us would get significantly worse.

One afternoon in the spring of 2018, Molly asked if I would take on some pre-production work in Orlando before heading to one of Golf Channel's most significant live events, which was something she occasionally requested. When she did, my boss didn't get too involved. As a contract employee, it was always nice to get the extra work, which meant extra money.

Not long after our verbal agreement, I received an out-of-the-blue email from my boss saying the promised rate would have to be reduced by over $1,000 because finance didn't approve it. Without hesitation, I emailed him back and asked if we could get Molly involved since she was his boss and the person who asked me to do the job in the first place. It only made sense to see if she could help. Instead of responding, he had a manager who worked underneath him call and tell me that if I didn't do the work at the new rate he offered, I would lose my position for that event. The tone was threatening, and the words were sharp. It was the first time I had ever been spoken to like that by anyone at Golf Channel.

Begrudgingly, I flew to Orlando to do the work at the reduced pay rate. As soon as I got there, my boss ordered me into his office, where he erupted, "Don't you ever think about going above me like that! Do you understand?"

No, I didn't understand, and I sure as hell didn't know how to respond. My heart was pounding. All I wanted to do was scream back at him, but I knew I couldn't. At this point, I wasn't sure where to turn. None of this made any sense...until it did. That's when the pieces of the puzzle started coming together.

By the following year, even though I had done everything I could to keep from rocking the boat with my boss,
the writing on the wall was starting to become apparent. I
was working a tournament in Birmingham when Sunday's
final round was extended to Monday because of bad weather.
In the golf world, this isn't too uncommon. As part of the
live television crew, we all do our best to accommodate the
extension, even without additional pay. But this particular
week, I had to get home for another contractual obligation. Keep in mind, there was nothing in my contract that
required me to stay. As I always did when an issue like this
happened, I informed my bosses that I couldn't stay and
ensured that my duties were covered before I left, which
had never been an issue in the previous 11 years.

The following day in Nashville, I received a phone
call informing me that one of the camera operators I had
prepped to fill in for me had misbehaved. According to the
PGA Tour rep who notified me, he rushed through the post-
round interview with the winner because he had a flight to
catch. It was deemed unprofessional behavior, and I was
part of the complaint since, apparently, I was responsible
for him to do the interview correctly even though I wasn't
the person who assigned him to do the job. Julie Lusk from
HR was copied on the email.

My boss called that same day and, once again, started
laying into me for what he said was a failure on my part.
I tried to defend myself by letting him know the amount
of time I'd taken with the person who would be staying in
my place before I left, going above and beyond what I was
asked to do to make sure things went well. But he wasn't
having any of it.

"I don't care that you were excused," he snipped. "How dare you leave! If you can't work a Monday finish, then don't take the show."

That rule, which never existed before, was subsequently implemented for me. Neither the camera guy nor my supervising producers who approved my leaving ever stood up for me, and I took the fall for all of them. Even then, I still didn't contact HR about the obvious smear campaign that was being built against me. I thought if I was tough enough, I would finally earn the respect I knew I deserved. That was my mistake.

A couple of months after the Monday finish episode, I was told that a tech manager had "called Orlando" and reported me to my bosses. He and I had what I thought was a minor disagreement over an editor taking a little extra time to edit a promo video for an event that our lead producer ordered.

As soon as I found out I had been reported, I approached him in the office to address the situation with him cordially. When I asked him if he'd turned me in, he immediately became combative, saying he didn't feel comfortable talking to me. When I pressed him about his unwillingness to explain himself, he responded with the unthinkable words mentioned earlier: "Because we live in a world where women and people of color rule the world. We just live in an HR world."

My stomach dropped. The most heart-wrenching part was that he genuinely believed that. He didn't trust me because I was a woman. Our female production manager was in the office with me when he said it. She looked uncomfortable but said nothing, even though I could tell she was just as shocked as me. My eyes welled up with tears, and I walked out of the office to avoid breaking down in front of them. I wanted to quit right then and there, but I knew that was precisely what he and my boss wanted. Still, I was too stunned and upset to think about calling HR.

One month later, I received an email from my boss informing me that I had committed another violation by having one of my kids with me at work during a recent tournament. To make it unequivocally clear: it was common-place for people to bring their families to work, especially during the summer. Beyond that, no rules stated we couldn't have them there. It wasn't some edict that was overlooked. Everyone did it.

Once this happened, my emotions did a 180. I went from being fearful of retaliation to pissed off at the obvious smear campaign they were waging against me. After reading the email, I contacted Julie Lusk and told her everything, including the earlier incidents with my boss. I wanted it documented that I felt targeted by my boss, and he appeared to be working at baselessly painting me as a bad employee.

Julie seemed sympathetic and said she would try to make things right. She asked if I wanted her to talk with my boss about my concerns. I begged her not to, knowing it would only enrage him. The main reason for reporting it to HR was to ensure I had my side of the story on record.

After a thorough HR investigation, the tech manager who said "we live in an HR world" was fired. Julie called to deliver the news, and I asked her if I should be concerned about retaliation. She assured me I was safe, but deep down, I couldn't help but worry. Imagine my disdain when I discovered that Julie most likely had revealed everything I said to those I complained about.

Later that year in October, when the time came to talk with management about negotiating a new contract, I sent my bosses an email asking to set up a time to speak. They never replied, and there was no doubt about it anymore. My time at Golf Channel was over.

Knowing in my gut that I was working one of my last tournaments in French Lick, Indiana, later that month, I said my goodbyes to the many close friends I had made on the road all those years. I told them I knew that was the last time we'd be working together. I was heartbroken, and so were they. When I got home, I received an email from my boss telling me we needed to talk by phone.

When he called, it was a cold and quick conversation. He said we needed to sever the relationship. When I asked why he was letting me go, he said it was because I had left early from a tournament the month prior. Of all the reasons he could've given, that one was the most preposterous because it was completely fabricated. To this day, it still upsets me to think about how he handled everything. It was a soul-crushing end to a job I loved deeply, where I made friendships I'll forever cherish.

I called Molly to tell her what had happened since she had always presented herself as a friend and mentor to me. I was hoping she would say or do something to help me feel better. Molly never returned that call. Finally, days later, she sent a tepid email claiming I had been let go for underwhelming performance issues. However, as if to cover all her political bases, she then pivoted and claimed that it wasn't necessarily the end for me there and that we'd have to wait and see what the future held. She also said she'd be a reference if I needed one. That was the last time we ever communicated. After years of what I thought was a friendship, Molly Solomon ghosted me, presumably, because I no longer served a purpose for her.

While all these events cut me deeply, I'm in a much better place now, teaching high school to kids who will hopefully one day be strong leaders with empathetic hearts and fair minds. I'm also grateful to be able to speak out about what I went through in hopes that it helps someone like me in the future. And I'm proud of Lisa and the other women for speaking up, too. It's hard to believe how similar our stories are, involving some of the same people.

All of these stories in the *Washington Post* article—Chelsea's, Jen's, plus the 16 other women who spoke out—broke my heart. But what was especially appalling was Ben's ultimate exposure of a toxic masculine boys' club culture that went all the way back to the beginning of Golf Channel. This threatening atmosphere didn't disappear when Comcast/NBCUniversal bought it, either. In some aspects, it only got worse.

Even after his article came out, Ben was left with unanswered questions. During an interview with the person who helped me write this book, Tucker Booth, on his podcast, Ben asked, "How does a culture allow for this to happen over and over again? Clearly, something was going on here. Even as far back as 2012, somebody thought it was okay to send these super, super sexually explicit emails (to a subordinate employee). Even when NBCUniversal took over the Golf Channel there was this trail of lawsuits, and they didn't sort of answer whether they needed to change the culture there or deal with that. How does it happen over and over again? Is there some sort of leadership or management breakdown that allows this to happen?"

Tucker followed those comments up by asking Ben whether he believed these systemic issues have always been a part of Golf Channel or if things got worse under Comcast/NBCUniversal's leadership. His response: "There was absolutely this wild, wild west culture that far predated NBC…there was this sort of male-driven culture and whether that changed with NBC…when you have that trail of lawsuits, I think if your company takes over a company like that, I think you have to do something. With my conversations with women who worked there, there wasn't a big change. [The bad behavior] was continuing from the days prior to NBC."

Shameful as all these findings are, it's not shocking when viewed from a distance. Ben found that Golf Channel started without clearly defined rules for male workplace behavior, and NBCUniversal did little to nothing to amend the murkiness when it took over. If anything, it seems that NBCUniversal handled all the disputes the same way it dealt with Matt Lauer's accusers. Management's motivation seemed to be more toward paying for women's silence than fixing a serious sexual harassment issue with their network star.

Once the *Washington Post* story was published, the power and reach of Ben's reporting exponentially multiplied the number of people who continued to contact me. Men and women shared their own stories of mistreatment and unseemliness. Here are just a few examples:

March 4, 2021

Hi Lisa, you probably don't remember me but I was on morning drive at the golf channel before the move. I'm sure you're facing some grief from people but I wanted to say thank you from the bottom of my heart for saying something about the injustices. That wash post article was beautiful (in the sad way it had to be). You are strong and you deserve to know how amazing you are. Keep your head up!

March 4, 2021

Heartfelt congratulations to you Lisa for getting the golf channel culture known to the public via *Washington Post* story. I worked at TGC for almost two years and left as even as a male I wasn't going to be in a work environment surrounding [me] where verbal and sexual harassment was going on. Amazed that culture never changed in 20 years. Wish you all the best in your future work/life endeavors Lisa!

March 4, 2021

Lisa! Thank you so much for sharing your story! I worked at NBC sports and (had) a very similar experience. In one situation a guy absolutely tormented me and made my life a living hell on a daily basis... He's still employed and continues to torment other women. We all knew HR was pointless so we stopped complaining and the toxic culture still remains. We all suffered in silence. So much gaslighting. I look forward to keeping an eye on the developing story at golf channel you brought forward to see things handled as they always should've been.

March 11, 2021

Hey Lisa, Just got your article forwarded to me and go you. I wondered what happened to you and glad to see you're doing something to hopefully change the Air of Assholism that gc exemplifies but sadly is prevalent throughout tv. Good luck!

To this day, people are still reaching out online and in person, thanking me for exposing the toxic culture at Golf Channel. My response to them is always the same: Speak out. Use your voice. It's the only way to make this better for women now and, more importantly, in the future.

CHAPTER 33

SOLIDARITY

THREE DAYS AFTER Ben Strauss' *Washington Post* article
was published, I was watching Sarah play in a golf tournament
in Ocala, Florida. Not long after her round began, my phone vibrated.
It was a text message from a woman I'd worked with for several
years at Golf Channel. Immediately, my feet stopped moving. I had a
hunch that this had something to do with the story. She'd forwarded
a screenshot of a Google Calendar invitation that she and the other
women who worked for the technical crew during the network's live
tournament coverage had all been sent earlier that day. The document
was titled "GC Women solidarity statement meeting" and included
these words:

> On Thursday we all read the *Washington Post* article
> and it immediately resonated with most of us who have
> experienced or witnessed in some form or another the claims
> made. We have an opportunity to lend public credibility
> to their stories and efforts to shed a light on something we
> all know to be pervasive at every level of the organization.

Tonight, we will share more details on how we can do this, in a discrete [manner]. We are encouraged by the response we have received from you all and are looking forward to seeing you and hearing your thoughts.

Then, in an accompanying text, the woman added to me personally, "It's just the beginning. We're all gonna talk tonight and come up with a statement that a legal team (on our side) will look over before we move forward but it's coming."

As soon as I read her message, a jolt of adrenaline ran through me. For years I'd dreamed of the day that women at Golf Channel would stop quietly complaining about the problems we faced, get organized, and start a movement demanding fair and equitable treatment at the network. Sexism shouldn't be an inevitable concession we had to make to work there. Retaliatory behavior, regardless of which gender it was being aimed at, was never justifiable or acceptable under any circumstance. Just like Rebecca Davis and her co-workers at NBC, when people unionized and worked to protect themselves legally, things inevitably began to change for the better.

A few days after I got back from Sarah's tournament in Ocala, I received another text from the woman who'd informed me about the Golf Channel solidarity statement meeting. This one was less exciting.

Well, several ladies showed up and several had hold ups between work and fear. In total we had 10 last night and are all gathering more friends to add a larger number to the group before publishing. But overall, I have to say I personally was disappointed in the fear level, and I believe the letter will come out but not as strong as I initially hoped. But that being said, I do think it will be a doorway for people like me and some of the others to tell the whole story soon after. Either way it's positively moving forward and will hope there's some traction along the way.

Once again, when it was time to act, many women who'd voiced their concerns about mistreatment backed off going to the meeting because they were scared it would blow back to the higher-ups. *Discouraging* isn't a strong enough word to describe the emotion attached to receiving news like this over and over again. It's demoralizing. Feeling unsafe for simply standing up for fair treatment at their job should *never* be a hazard that anyone is forced to navigate.

Still, despite the dispiriting news, 10 women did show up and vowed to rally others to join them. I decided to look at the glass as half-full and that their honest attempt to make things better wouldn't die on the vine. Something so admirable deserved to be considered.

Two days later, with ambiguity still swirling in the air, I received a far more hopeful text.

Just had communication end of day with GC where they acknowledged this is a serious problem and stated that they are open to having a dialogue and working with [us] to make real change. That being said, [she] is getting some feedback tomorrow on our statement in light of this positive feedback from GC. Our message will remain the same, but we may add something to recognize this willingness/ acknowledgement on their part, or it may remain just as it is without change. Anyway, our goal is to get it out on Friday at the latest.

The statement ended up being released the very next day, and their collective message was more powerful than I could've ever imagined:

Women of the Golf Channel Freelance Technical Crew Issues Statement of Solidarity

March 11, 2021

Twenty-four skilled craftswomen from all over the country, representing more than half the women on the technical crew, have joined in support of their co-workers. In this time of celebrating women, as the month of March celebrates Women's History Month, the women of the Golf Channel technical crew stand in solidarity with our sisters, Lisa Cornwell, Jen Johnson, Haley Zagoria, Chelsea Kite, and Laura Laytham, who so bravely told their stories to the *Washington Post.*

We are mothers, sisters, wives, and daughters with more than 550 years of live sports broadcast experience between us. Working alongside these courageous women who have come forward, we recognize there is not a single experience shared that we women on the freelance technical side have not also seen, heard, or personally experienced ourselves in our work at Golf Channel.

We believe that it is our duty and obligation to now lift up the voices of these women and echo their message. Their story is our story, and their truth is our truth.

Collectively, we call on Golf Channel to take appropriate measures to build a workplace of inclusion and equality. Sexist behavior has been permitted and protected by the highest levels of management at Golf Channel, creating a culture that has permeated to every level of their organization.

Recognizing and combating pervasive gender discrimination, ideologies, and sexual harassment requires more than just a training. Lasting cultural change must start at the top and weave its way down to the humblest of employees. Where problems exist, Golf Channel has indicated an openness to being a partner with the Union to achieve these goals. We look forward to this opportunity and hope to bear witness to timely implementation of policy and leadership decisions that will elevate more women, in all areas of the workforce, to more senior positions, and create pathways of upward mobility for the women of the technical crew, as well. ONLY these kinds of necessary changes, that include women at all levels, will prove the commitment Golf Channel has to creating a comfortable and inclusive environment for ALL people.

Creating a lasting environment of diversity, inclusivity, opportunity, and equal representation is what the women of the technical crafts at Golf Channel demand in this moment.

As powerful as the *Washington Post* article was on its own, this statement gave it even more legitimacy. Knowing how vital my response to it would be, I sought Tom's advice, once again, on the best way to publish it on my social media platforms. He encouraged me to hammer home how many women were now part of our collective crusade to force Golf Channel/NBC Sports to finally address the issues of unfair and inequitable treatment that so many women had been complaining about for years.

With that in mind, I quote-tweeted the union's statement of solidarity with these words:

> "Last week, 19 women revealed experiences of discrimination & retaliation by Golf Channel in the @WashingtonPost. Today, 24 more BRAVE women have joined us in speaking up. #43strong
> This statement is well worth your time to read—shedding more light on a culture that must change."

I'll forever be grateful to those women who had our backs when we needed them the most. Hopefully, this book can further ensure that these women and their contemporaries are respected and protected going forward.

CHAPTER 34

THE AFTERMATH

WHILE THERE WAS plenty to celebrate after I went on the *No Laying Up* podcast and the *Washington Post* article was published, there were a couple of times to follow that stopped me in my tracks. After the ANA Inspiration debacle, I was driving from Palm Springs to Los Angeles to catch a flight back to Orlando. Needing someone to talk to who understood how twisted the whole media landscape can be at times, especially toward women, I reached out to a respected female journalist I'd gotten to know fairly well over the years. There was no doubt in my mind that my absence from the final two rounds of a major championship would lead to all sorts of rumors and that Golf Channel would try to twist the incident and paint me as a bad employee. So I told her the entire story in an effort to protect myself as much as possible.

She told me that even though what happened was hard to believe, it still wasn't surprising. Before we hung up, she asked me to reach out once everything settled down, and we'd talk more. At the time, I felt comforted by her empathy and took hope in the fact that someone with her platform could help push back on Golf Channel and

Mizuno's inevitable upcoming smear campaign. I've always believed that women in the media needed to stick together, and this woman had been a loyal advocate. I was relieved to have her in my corner.

We didn't speak about my issues with Golf Channel again until almost 10 months later—well after I was no longer employed by the network. It was an accidental run-in at the KPMG Women's PGA Championship in Atlanta. I was there that week watching Sarah play, and she was working.

Back in January 2021, just weeks after my dismissal, this journalist made an appearance on Golf Channel, which wasn't out of the ordinary. She occasionally did live reports on the LPGA in the past, but those were usually on-site with a reporter. This time, however, it was different. She was in her house giving an update. The following week, she did it again…and then the week after that, and the week after that, and so on. It didn't take long to figure out this had become a regular gig.

So back to our accidental run-in in Atlanta. I was trying to find Sarah before her tee time that day when I spotted her. After a quick hello and casual, "How are you?" I brought up the pink elephant in the room—her weekly Golf Channel appearances. She paused, shook her head a little, and told me the part-time appearance contract with the network allowed her husband to quit his second job, which is the reason she accepted the offer. I told her it was okay, and I understood, which was completely honest. But I was also quick to point out that their motives for hiring her seemed pretty clear. The timing of it couldn't have served them any better. Not only did they add a woman to the payroll when all of these gender discrimination issues were coming out against them, but by bringing her onboard, they were essentially buying her silence.

I wasn't lying when I told her I didn't have any hard feelings. Truthfully, I don't blame her for accepting the offer. I probably would've done the same if roles had been reversed. It amplified her voice in the game and provided her with some extra income. But I still couldn't help thinking about how another strong woman had been muzzled by Golf Channel. This is what they do best and how they continue to get away with their misconduct.

Soon after Ben Strauss' *Washington Post* article came out, English professional golfer Meghan MacLaren published a blog on her website titled "For The Women." It was released on March 8, 2021, which was International Women's Day. Her heartfelt essay reads somewhat like a love letter, filled with gratitude and respect for the people who've inspired her to excel all these years while chasing a dream.

Celebrating everyone from the moms who sacrifice money and time to drive their kids to junior tournaments to the legendary greats of the game who paved the way for future generations, Meg made a point of giving extensive credit where it's undoubtedly due. She also boldly took on many of the challenges and inequities still facing women in golf.

Early in the article, she wrote, "Our chances of success today—success being based on our achievements and skills rather than our gender or appearance—arise from the women who have come before us. Thanks to the efforts of innumerable people, those chances are increasing. But in both society as a whole and its microcosm of the golfing world, we still have a way to go."

Meg then highlighted a jarring financial stat that's hard to accept logically: "There are 70 players on the PGA Tour career money list with higher career earnings than the leading LPGA career earner. That LPGA player happens to be one of the most dominant athletes of all time. She has won more majors in the women's game than 69 of those 70 players have won in the men's game."

The dominant female player she references is Annika Sorenstam. Over her stellar career, Annika won 72 LPGA Tour titles, including ten major championships. Additionally, she earned eight Player of the Year honors and remains the only woman to shoot a 59 in competition. Yet she trails 70 men in career earnings who, except for Tiger Woods, haven't come close to her success level. That's hard to fathom.

Soon after Meg touched on pay inequality, she gave credit to some "powerful" women in golf who are pushing to even the score, and surprisingly, it included me: "For the ones in power, breaking through glass ceiling after glass ceiling while protecting others from the shards of glass as they shatter. Becca Hembrough and Alex Armas and Lisa Cornwell, leading the way loudly and unapologetically because they have no reason not to. Because they understand what leadership sounds like—and it isn't silence."

I was honored by this mention, to say the least, and took it as a true sign that my mission to expose the gender inequities at Golf Channel and the entire sport was making an impact. With that in mind, imagine my surprise when, four months later, the week of the AIG Women's Open championship, an edited version of Meg's blog resurfaced on the R&A's tournament website. Considering the R&A is one of only two governing bodies for the entire game of golf globally, the changes they made were significant.

The first massive omission was the paragraph about the 70 PGA Tour players who've earned more career money than Annika Sorenstam. It was cut out as though the information was somehow unimportant. As bothersome as that exclusion was, my jaw dropped to the floor when I read the paragraph that originally included my name, only to notice it'd been removed as well. Becca Hembrough and Alex Armas were still mentioned. In fact, all the other words in the paragraph were printed verbatim except for *Lisa Cornwell*.

Sarah and I were home when the R&A's version of Meg's article was published. Neither of us could believe this had happened, Sarah even more so than me. At first, I thought maybe I'd missed something. *Perhaps they moved some names around*, I thought. So

I reread it. Unfortunately, this wasn't an oversight. Ironically, I'd just been erased from a story honoring women's influence in the golf world.

My initial reaction was more dejection than anger. How could a highly respected governing body like the R&A, which certainly knew that such an obvious slight could potentially damage its reputation, willingly sign off on censoring my name?

Without delay, I posted this tweet, tagging the AIG Women's Open, and displayed screenshots of the censored and uncensored versions of Meg's essay side by side.

> I've spent years advocating for FAIRNESS & EQUALITY in women's golf.
> Dear @AIGWomensOpen, You have some explaining to do.
> Why remove my name & the pay equality paragraph in Meg MacLaren's article → one she wrote for #International WomensDay?

Sarah and I had an early tee time that day. But once I posted the tweet, she told me I should stay home because she was convinced I'd be contacted by all sorts of people about the R&A's slight. Even though I had my doubts, I decided she may be right and sent her off to play without me.

That day, besides a few sympathetic friends, no one reached out to discuss it on or off the record. It was as if the blatant whitewashing didn't matter, or it was too risky for anyone to touch. Either way, it reinforced some of the discouragement I already felt.

That feeling of dejection would soon turn into a strong sense of righteous indignation. Someone needed to answer for this, and that person was R&A CEO Martin Slumbers. Since the buck stopped with him, Slumbers had the final say on the revisions to Meg's essay. I wanted to be sure he acknowledged my concerns, so I sent him an official letter by mail with a tracking number. That way, there was no chance the R&A could claim my letter was lost in the mail or never delivered if only sent via email.

These were my words to Slumbers:

Dear Mr. Slumbers,

I hope this letter finds you well. While we have not met personally, I am well aware of your long-standing commitment to grow the game of golf and your recent initiatives to elevate girls and women in our sport. For that, I applaud you.

I am writing in regard to an article that was written by Meghan MacLaren and posted on her website on March 8, 2021, in celebration of International Women's Day. As is typical with any article Meg writes, her words are thoughtful, powerful and eloquently on point. I was particularly moved to be among the names she mentioned to illustrate the journey of women in golf.

For the ones in power, breaking through glass ceiling after glass ceiling while protecting others from the shards of glass as they shatter. Becca Hembrough and Alex Armas and Lisa Cornwell, leading the way loudly and unapologetically because they have no reason not to. Because they understand what leadership sounds like—and it isn't silence.

This past week, the article was reposted by the AIG Women's Open. Can you imagine my surprise and disappointment when I discovered that my name had been removed, as well as an equal pay paragraph with statistics comparing women's professional golf to the PGA Tour?

Meg MacLaren is a person of high character and so am I, which is exactly why she included me. I am very proud to lend my voice and my efforts to elevate women, especially women in golf and golf broadcasting. To say that I am disheartened over the changes that were made to Meg's article would be an understatement.

When I grew up, it was the British Open and the Women's British, and I never missed a minute of it. And now I am writing to the CEO of the R&A because your organization deemed me somehow unworthy to be included on a list that was thoughtfully chosen. It is an article from a professional golfer's website expressing her unedited feelings on important issues, as we celebrated a day elevating women. It was borrowed…and then subsequently changed.

So my simple question is this: Why would the R&A do such a thing?

I believe it is not only a fair question to ask, but also worthy of an answer that is as thoughtful as her article. I trust you will agree.

Respectfully,

Lisa Cornwell

Sure enough, and somewhat to my surprise, Martin Slumbers did send a personal response to my letter. The short, vague reply tap-danced around any straight answers to my inquiries, though, and instead used brevity as an avoidance tactic. The politically correct language carefully diverted attention away from the R&A's censorship, instead acting as if its actions were to preserve some sort of impartiality.

The only reasonably telling portion of his reply came near the end:

I have taken the opportunity to understand more of the background from The R&A's perspective and am now in a position to explain the sequence of events, for clarity. In fact, the article was originally commissioned by The R&A from Meghan McLaren [sic] to coincide with International

Women's Day on 8 March, to be published as part of a range
of content in support of IWD. It was requested from her
and then edited with her knowledge. We reserve the right
to edit content for our own channels and in our role as a
global governing body, to retain neutrality.

This was the best Martin Slumbers could do, branding their
actions as an attempt to act neutral. Highlighting the mind-boggling
pay disparity between the PGA and LPGA Tours is a matter of fact. No
side was taken when Meg wrote those lines. She simply said progress
was still needed for female golfers to reach the financial heights their
male counterparts already had. She cast no aspersions on the PGA
Tour or men in general. All Meg MacLaren did was make a compelling case for progress.

As far as leaving my name out was concerned, let me reiterate
that my issue has never been with men in general, just the handful of
powerful men (and two women) who made working at Golf Channel so difficult. None of that was mentioned when Meg included my
name. The only neutrality that could conceivably be preserved would
be between the R&A and its corporate pals at NBCUniversal.

Slumbers ended his letter with these debatably disingenuous
sentiments:

> As you point out in your letter, The R&A is a champion of
> women's golf and it is our passionate desire to see greater
> recognition for professional women golfers, who are role
> models for bringing more women and girls into our sport
> to help it thrive in future. That is clearly a desire you share.
> There was certainly no intention on The R&A's part to dis-
> hearten you in the way you describe in your letter and I
> am sorry you were made to feel that way. I hope that we

can put this matter behind us as we all pursue what's best for the sport.

Whether their intention was to "dishearten" me or not, it was undoubtedly to erase me from public view. Considering that everything I've done since I started speaking out has been to recognize women in golf and the media, none of his reply rang even somewhat sincere. It was just another powerful person trying to cover himself and the organization he represents.

To Meg's credit, she wasn't deterred. My name remains in the original essay on her website, and it still humbles me to read those words today. It's one of the many parts of this journey that's kept me moving forward, more convinced than ever before of the powerful force that our collective voices do indeed have on the world today.

CHAPTER 35

EEOC, PART III

WITH SO MUCH inflammatory information against Golf Channel and NBC Sports continuing to roll in after the podcast, Tom reached out to our EEOC investigator in multiple emails. He relayed the news that immediately following the podcast's release, I'd been contacted by scores of women, thanking me for speaking out and relating even more awful accounts of workplace mischief. He wisely wanted this documented on the record.

Quoting Tom:

> Those stories include a female producer who found out that all three of her similarly situated male colleagues were being paid salaries that were at least two times her salary; a senior female employee walking in on Brandel Chamblee and a male colleague while they were discussing (and continued to discuss) which LPGA pro on the tour they were covering *had the nicest breasts*; as well as at least a half dozen similar, verifiable stories—most of which made me cringe. FYI, I also interviewed a female former TGC employee who was

present, along with Lisa, when a TGC colleague shared with them that Brandel Chamblee had said he'd been speaking to Executive Producer Molly Solomon for quite some time "about getting rid of Lisa."

This update went on to mention that after the *No Laying Up* podcast, I was contacted by Ben Strauss at the *Washington Post*, who'd interviewed many of the women, and that his article was due to be released within a week or so.

Tom also noted that Golf Channel had been dishonest about George Savaricas undergoing the same "transition" that I was and that he was still regularly hosting events on Golf Channel even after I'd left. He mentioned that, while I'd been supposedly let go for budgetary reasons, a new female reporter and former Miss America, Kira Dixon, had been hired and was already reporting at PGA Tour events.

A few months later, we filed our second charge with the EEOC. The first charge cited discrimination and retaliation involving the demotion. The second charge cited discrimination and retaliation as well, but this time it was tied to the non-renewal of my contract.

As expected, the lawyer NBCUniversal assigned to my original case, Temitope Yusuf, sent a reply to our second official filing with the EEOC. Even with the mounting evidence that kept piling up against Golf Channel, NBCUniversal didn't change its tune one bit. Instead, it was digging in even deeper this time, claiming that my speaking out publicly was a toothless smear campaign. (Just wait until she reads this book!) Ms. Yusuf again deemed the discrimination charges were untrue and dismissed our compelling evidence of retaliation.

As before, Ms. Yusuf labeled my performance at Golf Channel as below average. There was a vague accusation of me not following a manager's instructions regarding my interviewing style. Reading this reply was absolute déjà vu. Wasn't it Einstein who said the definition of insanity is doing the same thing repeatedly and expecting different results? Whether or not NBCUniversal was "insane" to stick with its redundant pattern of character assassination, it was still irritating to keep reading all the lies and awful things she was saying about me.

Ms. Yusuf then dismissed our claims that Golf Channel had continued to employ George Savaricas full-time. Using semantics, she pushed back, stating that he and I were both still eligible for employment, so we were wrong. She went back to the old refrain that all those downsizing moves were due to budget cuts and Golf Channel's recent move of their headquarters from Orlando to Stamford, Connecticut. To discredit the accusations of ageism and sexism, Ms. Yusuf mentioned that two women under the age of 40 had also been let go or had their roles downsized.

When the issue of Golf Channel hiring Kira Dixon to replace me arose, Ms. Yusuf outright denied that she was my replacement. Instead, she characterized her as just a freelance employee who was part of a carousel of available reporters—men and women. Using this flimsy logic, she dismissed my accusations as unclear and irrelevant.

As previously stated in NBCUniversal's first rebuttal, Ms. Yusuf affirmed I couldn't prove that gender, age, or retaliation were factors in Golf Channel's decision to move on from me. She again laid all the blame at the feet of budget cuts and my lack of professionalism and beseeched the EEOC investigators to drop all charges against them.

The pendulum-like effect of swinging back and forth between claiming their budget was too tight and then knocking me professionally was starting to test my nerves. It seemed like Golf Channel/ NBCUniversal was still banking on the fact that I didn't have enough resources and mental wherewithal to see the case through to its cryptic conclusion. But I knew something they didn't.

After I'd paid Tom's initial retainer and then a second installment (which he didn't even ask for), he stopped billing me his hourly rate. According to Tom, that was because he believed in my case, knew I couldn't afford his typical rate, and had come to view me as a virtual sister. For the past two years, Tom's generously given his time to my cause, and I most likely would've given up hope without his unselfish love and support. Words could never express how grateful I am for men like him. He's a true people's champion.

———————

In our final submission to the EEOC, Tom and my cousin Allison went to work right away on debunking the notion that I hadn't met the burden of proof to show that Golf Channel had discriminated against me over age, gender, and class-protected status. Allison offered to help because she knew my entire story better than anyone and also knew that Tom wasn't charging me anymore and wanted to take some of the workload off his plate. Unlike our previous response, where Tom jabbed at NBCUniversal's lawyers for their disrespectful tone, he and Allison threw nothing but pinpoint punches at the facts themselves this time.

Four different factors need to be met legally to prove that discrimination had occurred in any case like mine. First, that I was a member of a protected class (age, gender, and sexual orientation-wise). Second, that I was qualified for the work. Third, that I suffered an adverse employment action. Lastly, that I was displaced by a person outside of my protected class.

In our final response, one that my cousin spent hours crafting, she laid it all out succinctly:

> Not even TGC disputes that Ms. Cornwell meets factors one
> and three. Although the fourth factor was not addressed
> in TGC's Second Position Statement, Ms. Cornwell was

displaced by someone outside of her protected classes. First, with respect to age discrimination, TGC hired twenty-nine-year-old Kira Dixon in 2021, who is a tournament reporter for TGC. This is a position that Ms. Cornwell held during her tenure at TGC and is currently qualified to perform. Accordingly, after TGC terminated Ms. Cornwell's employment, they hired an individual outside of Ms. Cornwell's age-protected class.

Second, regarding Ms. Cornwell's gender discrimination claim, she was also displaced by an individual outside of her protected class. Specifically, although TGC claims that Ms. Cornwell and George Savaricas…were treated in a similar fashion regarding their contracts, Mr. Savaricas continued his employment with TGC in 2021, with his role and exposure at TGC exponentially greater in 2021. TGC may not have entered into a formal contract with Mr. Savaricas in 2021, but he engaged in more tournaments and on-air time in 2021 as compared to 2020, all while Ms. Cornwell did not.

Based on the foregoing undisputed facts, Ms. Cornwell was replaced by someone outside of her gender-protected class when TGC terminated her contract in 2020.

Finally, with respect to the second factor set forth in McDonnell Douglas/Webb-Edwards—whether Ms. Cornwell was qualified to do her job—TGC actually concedes this factor in TGC's Second Position Statement by stating that (since Lisa was currently still a theoretically employable person) if she is qualified to work as a freelance reporter for TGC…it refers to Mr. Savaricas as Ms. Cornwell's "counterpart" qualified to do the job for which she was not renewed.

Allison then offered an extensive definition of what retaliation is under the law. To paraphrase, it's when someone endures an adverse action that keeps them from performing duties for which they are utterly qualified. As before in our submissions, we again presented all the evidence about the numerous times I'd spoken truth to power, which had indeed incensed Mark Summer, Adam Hertzog, Geoff Russell, Brandel Chamblee, and Molly Solomon.

One by one, Allison explained how this was a systematic chain of events that indeed violated my class-protected rights and ended up in an adverse position that negatively affected my employment. She covered all the same situations that have been laid out throughout this book, including my run-ins with Mark Summer, Brandel Chamblee, Geoff Russell, and (vicariously) Molly Solomon. The fact that George Savaricas and Kira Dixon continued to fill my roles (as well as get consistent work) was resurrected. She also zeroed in on the ANA/Mizuno fiasco and the ensuing fallout. To act like there hadn't been an adverse effect on me mentally and professionally was lunacy.

Once she had the legal puzzle pieces perfectly put together, Tom concluded her masterpiece rebuttal with this knockout punch:

> Ms. Cornwell has met her burden of proof with respect to her age and gender discrimination claim as well as her claim of retaliation. As we have shown in this Informational Supplement, TGC has fallen far short of rebutting these claims with its ever-changing, inconsistent explanations— all of which lack evidentiary support and most of which are squarely contrary to irrefutable evidence: (a) characterizing Ms. Cornwell's job performance as (not good) despite complementary written performance reviews chocked full of accolades; TGC's failure to explain the suspicious absence of performance reviews during the time frame when TGC was primed to retaliate against her; TGC's puzzling assertion that Ms. Cornwell could still work (as an employee) after TGC supposedly kicked her to the curb for poor job

performance; and (d) TGC replacing Ms. Cornwell with a much younger female employee and a male employee whose employment status was falsely characterized in TGC's initial response to Ms. Cornwell's First Charge of Discrimination and Retaliation.

Allison and Tom nailed these ridiculous counterclaims to the ground. Citing factual intelligence that's impossible to dispute, they drove the point home that (no matter what NBCUniversal said) I was being aggressed upon by a retaliatory, discriminatory business regime dead bent on seeing me drummed out of TV.

CHAPTER 36

CASE CLOSED

OCTOBER 14, 2022. The email arrived in my inbox early that afternoon. It was actually two separate emails—one for each case. 942 days had passed since we filed our first charge with the EEOC on the heels of my demotion. And it'd been 480 days since we filed the additional charge when my contract wasn't renewed.

The EEOC sent its official notifications that it'd reached a decision not to pursue my cases any further and instead had issued a 'Right to Sue' letter for each charge. This essentially gave me the green light to proceed with a federal lawsuit—albeit at my own expense. Once you receive this type of notification, you have 90 days from the date issued to file in court.

A woman named My Linh Kingston from the Tampa Field Office was the investigator originally assigned to my cases. Tom communicated with her fairly regularly from the get-go. He and I also had a couple of lengthy calls with her during the early and intermediate stages of the investigation. Ms. Kingston seemed eager to learn more and said she wanted to hear my side of the story. According to Tom, credibility plays a key role in cases like these, so I welcomed any opportunity for us to all talk directly.

Ms. Kingston asked intelligent questions, which gave us both the impression that she was indeed taking my accusations seriously. Tom told me that an EEOC investigation like mine would typically take, on average, six to nine months before a decision was made. However, due to the COVID-19 pandemic, we had to account for it potentially taking longer than expected. Little did we know how much longer we'd actually have to wait.

After a year and a half had passed from our initial filing, Tom began reaching out to Ms. Kingston by email to get an update on where the EEOC stood with my cases. He didn't get a response. A couple more months passed when Tom tried to contact her again. And again, silence. It appeared as though this woman we'd put our faith in was now ghosting us, which didn't make any sense at all.

Finally, Tom was contacted out of the blue by a new EEOC investigator named Jesus Gonzalez in July of 2022. In a stunning turn of events, we were informed that Ms. Kingston was no longer working on my cases and had failed to upload several important documents in their system. This explained why we hadn't heard anything from her or the EEOC in over nine months.

Mr. Gonzalez was under the assumption that we'd declined to respond to NBCUniversal's last rebuttal, which was obviously inaccurate. The final response that Allison and Tom drafted was 81 pages in length and included numerous case citings to back up my claims of discrimination and retaliation. Then, something even more bizarre happened. Somehow my private case information was sent to one of Tom's other clients who was embroiled in her own discrimination case with the EEOC. *How in the world could this be happening, especially so late in the ballgame?* I asked myself.

Tom recalls it this way: "...The new investigator [Mr. Gonzalez] somehow used another client's email, thinking it was mine, to start sending me emails saying we hadn't ever responded to Golf Channel's response. In fact, the first investigator [Ms. Kingston] confirmed via email on October 27, 2021, that she had received our response. You can imagine how embarrassed the new investigator was when I forwarded him all the emails from October explaining that [Kingston] was using an email for the charging party in an unrelated EEOC charge filed on June 7th [2021]. This didn't give me a lot of confidence in the EEOC."

Once Mr. Gonzalez finally received the misplaced information, he promised to get back to us with some sort of resolution as soon as possible. As upsetting as it was to find out how badly the EEOC had botched my cases, I still held onto a flicker of hope that somehow they'd make it right. Then, three more months passed with no communication whatsoever.

Now, after more than two and a half years after our initial filing, the EEOC found my cases to have merit but, for whatever reason, didn't want to be involved. Given the late blunders and missteps, plus considering how long the cases had been dangling out there, it appeared the easiest thing to do was close them without any further investigation and put it (and their mistakes) behind them. Mr. Gonzalez never once did what you'd think any new investigator assigned to multiple charges of discrimination and retaliation with credible evidence to back up those claims would do—he never asked Tom or me a single question about anything related to my charges.

To this day, no one from the EEOC has ever acknowledged or apologized for their gross mismanagement of leaking my personal information to someone else. And it makes me wonder how many others who've endured workplace violations like mine—or worse—have slipped through the cracks because it wasn't worth the agency's time.

As of the writing of this chapter, I'm still mulling my options. I obviously want Golf Channel to be held accountable for what they've done, but I have to consider the bigger picture, too. While I've already acknowledged how generous Tom's been with his time and expertise, it's still cost me almost $15,000 just to get this far, and a lawsuit could rack up a bill 20 to 30 times that amount, or even higher. Another factor to consider is that I'd have to get another lawyer because Tom isn't licensed to practice in the state of Florida, which is where the lawsuit would have to be filed. The thought of starting over with someone else representing me is daunting, to say the least.

Once the EEOC cases seemed to be in a perpetual game of legal limbo, I became determined not to let up or stay silent, which was the motivating factor in writing this book. Otherwise, what would stop the same people from committing the same heinous violations again and again?

———————

Like many in my current position, it's easy to overreact and think somehow the EEOC's handling of my grievance was personally aimed at me. But by doing some digging online I soon realized that my underwhelming experience with the agency's investigators was far too common. In fact, since the EEOC's inception in the 1970s, it's had to weather a lingering reputation of being a "Toothless Tiger."

In a 2021 investigative report by Fast Company, author Pavithra Mohan sums up the EEOC's fiscal flaws this way: "As of 2020, the agency is more understaffed than it has been in decades, and it's reeling from changes that were introduced under the Trump administration. In 1980, the EEOC had a staff of 3,390; by last year, that number had been slashed by more than 40%, leaving its workforce at just 1,939 employees."

Cathy Ventrell-Monsees, a senior adviser to three EEOC chairs, recalled it as follows to Mohan: "The EEOC has always faced challenges. Not enough budget. Not enough staff. An overwhelming number of charges. The system and structures they put in place were really not meant to investigate and resolve the majority of charges, in part because of the burden of the volume of charges."

This has led the EEOC to issue many right-to-sue letters like mine while declining to further pursue the charges themselves. The Fast Company article speculates that many of our cases are not tried because they aren't slam dunks. If that is indeed the truth, how incredibly discouraging it is to know that (again) the government agency created to protect employee rights is resistant to taking on tough cases.

So how do problems of discrimination and retaliation get better in the workplace without proper oversight and true legal protection? Unfortunately, it isn't illegal to be an asshole, and there are plenty of them out there.

This is why leadership matters. Companies need leaders and managers who care about the culture of their workplace and will do everything within their power to keep this toxic behavior at bay. When you have an employee who's constantly creating mayhem, you have to put a stop to it. By allowing bullies to get away with obvious misbehavior, you're creating a firestorm of problems that only encourages others to follow suit. It also keeps people from speaking up about similar situations out of their own fears of backlash.

Trust me, I know both of these scenarios all too well.

CHAPTER 37

LESSONS LEARNED

———

No matter what happens, or how bad it seems today, life does go on, and it will be better tomorrow.

—Maya Angelou

I'LL BE HONEST, it didn't cross my mind at the beginning of this journey to include a "Lessons Learned" chapter in the book. My attitude when this project started was *they have the lessons to learn, not me.* But the more I've written, reflected, and talked to others and myself, the more I've realized this has been an excellent opportunity for some personal growth, too. I'm well aware that I'm nowhere close to perfect, and that I've made my fair share of mistakes along the way. While I may not be as easily triggered as I once was, it can still happen from time to time, depending on the situation. I've always been a steadfast defender of people, including myself, but I realize now that you can be a defender without being defensive. As cliché as it may sound, the best thing I've tried to do is recognize my mistakes, own them, learn from them and, most importantly, not repeat them.

When I went on the *No Laying Up* podcast in January 2021, I was angry. I've never been one to hide my emotions, so I didn't think twice about letting out every bit of that fury as I told my story publicly for the first time. As you might expect, there were some naysayers who called me a "disgruntled former employee" after listening to what I had to say. By definition, I suppose they were right—but not in the way those words are typically meant when used together. I wasn't *disgruntled* because I'd been let go. I was *disgruntled* because of how so many other women and I were treated.

This whole process has taught me that words matter in a way I never quite realized before, including my own. Looking back, I outwardly expressed and held on to a lot of that anger a bit longer than I probably should have. Yes, I'm still miffed by all that happened at Golf Channel, especially how it ended. But I no longer have this burning desire to bury them with my words. Now, it's more about justice and protecting the young women who are just starting to make their way into the workforce.

A big part of writing this book was the unavoidable task of reliving everything that had happened over the years, which included pouring through hundreds of emails, texts, and documents I'd collected for our EEOC charges. Every time I go back and reread one of the scathing responses the NBCUniversal legal team sent to the EEOC, bashing my job performance *and* my character, I can still feel some of those old heated emotions start to surface again. But then I remind myself they only did it because they had nothing else to go on. They have no documentation of poor performances or anything that remotely proves I wasn't a supportive co-worker and fully committed to my job.

I've been able to let go of the need to respond to every hateful person on Twitter who attacks me for things they know nothing about, and I've tried my best not to use condemning words that would give them any opportunity to come after me personally. Although you can't completely avoid the detractors, you can keep them at bay, and I try my best to do that now because, quite frankly, it isn't worth the headache. Through it all, I've finally accepted that I can't control what people say or how they react to me. I can only control how I respond to them, which was a lesson I definitely needed to learn—for my own sanity. Trust me; this book contained many more four-letter words in the beginning than in the final manuscript. My cousin helped me realize that I didn't have to point any fingers. All I had to do was tell the story honestly and let you, the reader, decide for yourself. Hopefully, I've achieved that goal.

This whole process has been cathartic in many ways, and I sleep much better at night and feel more at peace than I have for a long time. I've also been able to spend more time at home and at tournaments with Sarah, including occasionally caddying for her—something that never would've been allowed if Golf Channel still employed me. Being a professional athlete can be incredibly lonely at times, especially in an individual sport. So it's been a huge blessing for us both. And selfishly, it still keeps me involved in the game at a high level and close to the players and caddies on the LPGA Tour who I've gotten to know so well over the years. I worked hard to build those relationships, and I'm grateful to still have them as friends.

Speaking of friends, this experience has taught me who my true friends are and why it matters. I read a quote a couple of months ago, and it really hit home: "Being an ally only when it's comfortable and convenient for you is absolutely not being an ally." Sadly, I lost a few "friends" who I thought were allies soon after I spoke out. Whatever the reason, I'm happy to say that I'm doing my best not to make assumptions anymore. It creates way too much negative energy, and I no longer want to be in that headspace. I want to embrace life with the people who matter most to me. And hopefully, we can do some good with this book. I've said it quite often over the past couple of years but as crazy as it may sound, I think I was destined to do exactly what I'm doing right now. Not everyone has the financial ability (thank you, Sarah, for letting me take a year off to work on this book) or the support at home to go through it. And trust me, it takes both. A fight like this can beat you down in a hurry. I've been fortunate enough to have what I've needed to overcome it, and I realize not everyone's that lucky. This battle is for all the women who wanted to step into the ring to take on these perpetrators, but their place in life, for whatever reason, didn't allow them to do it.

Even though I've lost potential job opportunities in the media or haven't been asked to participate in some high-profile events that I've always done in the past, there's some real change taking place. Mizuno now spends money to support LPGA players at their tournaments. More women are being used in Golf Channel's live tournament broadcasts and in the studio—even though there's still a long way to go. The women in the field (audio, video, technical operators) who've felt slighted for years have been in talks with Golf Channel/NBC Sports about improvements that can be made regarding equality in assignments and pay.

While I don't pat myself on the back for these changes, I do feel as though I've contributed a little something that's important to this world. My goal now is to keep the conversation going. We must continue to educate people on why the way we treat people matters. We must continue to press for fair and equal treatment. It takes a village to do that—especially our village of women who've been forced into silence for far too long.

As for what's next, that's an important question I'm still trying to answer. Life's pushed me in this direction for a reason, and I don't plan on backing down because there's a lot of work still to do. While Golf Channel may have taken away my job, they could never—and will never—take away my voice. I fully expect some of the people mentioned in this book and their flock of friends or followers to come after me. That's fine. But they'll never influence or control my narrative.

A trusted friend asked me recently if I was worried about being canceled. I laughed and told her I thought that happened a long time ago. If you're making waves as a woman, there will always be a significant group of people who write you off immediately and do their best to break you emotionally. The truth is, not only am I ready for it, but I welcome it. As Natalie Maines so boldly said in the documentary *Shut Up & Sing*, which details the many obstacles The Chicks had to overcome after being canceled by country radio...

Bring. It. On.

AFTERWORD

FROM TUCKER'S LENS

I **FIRST CONNECTED WITH** Lisa on January 1, 2021. As you
have now read, that was also the day she sent out her tweet heard
around the golf world. Like a large chunk of our society, I have been
hooked on Twitter for years, especially Golf Twitter. One of the things
that stands out the most on Golf Twitter is when someone takes a
loud, controversial stance, especially when it's aimed at the golf world's
golden geese. Besides conflict pimps like Brandel Chamblee, I would
say that most of the golf media world is conflict averse. Firing shots
as loud as Lisa's were that day was borderline shocking to see online.
It also immediately piqued my interest in her story; I wanted to learn
more about the alleged misdeeds at Golf Channel.

As soon as I saw her tweet, I followed Lisa. To my pleasant surprise, within minutes, she followed me back. I wondered if it had
anything to do with the fact that we had both covered the 2019 Farmers Insurance Open in San Diego or possibly my *Rappers Don't Golf*
podcast, since she had recently liked a tweet I'd posted with a link to
an interview with her former Golf Channel colleague Karen Stupples.
Feeling emboldened by all of it, I sent Lisa the following DM:

Hi Lisa—you won't remember me, but I was in the media tent with you at the Farmers last year. Always been a huge admirer of your work. Thanks for the follow. It's still a thrill when the folks I look up to follow me on here. Reaching out because I saw your post about being more vocal about women's rights issues in the workplace. I have a podcast I host that has featured a number of your GC colleagues: Jerry Foltz, Karen Stupples, Frank Nobilo, Terry Gannon, Matt Ginella, and many more. I would love to interview you about your life/career and any other topics you'd like (including equality in the workplace.)

Ten minutes later, Lisa replied, "Hi Tucker! Of course, I remember you. Text or email me and we'll figure it out. Would love to do it. Happy New Year!"

She left her cell number and email address, and we set up a time to chat by phone. The day we first spoke, I thought we were just touching base to set up her interview on the podcast. Instead, she immediately pivoted and told me that she had been researching my work online and found "I Built a Masterpiece and Then I Fell Apart," a biographical profile piece I'd written about Golf Channel creator Michael J. Whelan.

"Tucker, within the first few paragraphs of reading your Whelan profile, the hair on the back of my neck stood up. I knew right then and there that you're the person I want to help me write my book. I knew it immediately."

I was thrilled. Not only was I getting my first big opportunity to break into the literary world, but I was also being tasked with helping Lisa Cornwell battle Golf Channel/NBCUniversal. Having just recently read Ronan Farrow's deftly written book *Catch and Kill,* I was well aware of the toxic masculinity and retaliatory culture that still seems so pervasive at NBC.

As a subsidiary of NBCUniversal, I could imagine Golf Channel being just as embroiled in the alleged misconduct. If anything, the idea of battling the same people who had tacitly enabled Matt Lauer and Harvey Weinstein to avoid being outed for their crimes seemed almost fun. There is little in life I enjoy more than speaking truth to power. It's why I will probably never be employable in the mainstream media. But, no matter what, it put me in the perfect position to help Lisa. Neither of us wanted to work for people like that anyway.

With me in her corner, we were poised to at least make a dent in NBCUniversal's armor. Moreover, we could work together to spread the message: everyone (especially women and minorities) needs to be willing to stand up and hold people accountable when they see wrongdoing in the world. This type of "troublemaking" is essential in the workplace. Unless decent people bravely apply pressure on those higher-ups who keep getting away with their crimes, nothing will ever change for the better.

I imagine many readers wonder why Lisa chose a man to co-write her book, especially considering her focus on women's rights. I can't speak for her directly on this issue, but I can tell you why I care about workplace discrimination like the kind Lisa describes within. While I have never experienced much of any sexism aimed at me, the two women closest to me—my wife and my mom—have had to endure plenty of it professionally. They have dealt with more than their fair share of unwarranted flak, from inappropriate actions and language to blatantly disrespectful behavior. Much of the drama involved voicing unpopular opinions and being shackled with blame after speaking out.

When Lisa and I began writing the book proposal for *Troublemaker,* we spent hours on the phone, recording every conversation, no matter how long. Lisa would exhaustively revisit and detail many of her life's most personally devastating moments. At one point, she half-jokingly quipped that I knew more about her than anyone besides Sarah. She even doubled down, confiding that I probably had heard more about her deep, dark secrets than she had even told her parents. I felt honored that she trusted me enough to be so open. I also immediately began to feel the heat. This book had to be done right, or else the peanut gallery would eviscerate Lisa and me.

For those who don't know, as a writer, I'm more of an investigative journalist than a puff-piece kind of guy. I'm good at digging dirt, not simply because I want to know my subject's shortcomings, but because without them, I can't paint a complete picture of them. Regardless of how great they are at their given gifts, the ugly side of people drives them just as much as the bright side. Examining the skeletons in one's closet helps to elucidate their motivations and explain why they react to life the way they do. I'm also fascinated by my subjects, hungry to know every juicy detail like any overzealous observer.

With that in mind, I needed to be sure Lisa was on that level before putting my professional reputation on the line. She sounded credible when we spoke, but I needed to know if there was a vastly different side to her story. So, I started the excavation process, reaching out to all my contacts at Golf Channel, vetting Lisa's version of things versus their recollections. One after another, everyone but Matt Ginella verified that Lisa was a great journalist and gracious co-worker.

Many affirmed that she was a tough girl who wasn't afraid to speak her mind but was never cruel or intolerable in any way. All of them confirmed that she had been shitcanned at the end. One offhand exclamation from an on-course cameraman during the 2021 U.S. Open at Torrey Pines summed it succinctly to me: "Man…they really fucked her!"

It should also be noted that no one I spoke to came to the defense of Brandel Chamblee, Matt Ginella, Molly Solomon, or Geoff Russell. Across the board, they all agreed that the four of them were snakes and not to be trusted. They also made it clear that they could not go on the record with any critical comments because they wanted to protect their jobs. Though they may have loved Lisa, at the end of the day, they had to protect their paycheck. Understandable as that may be, it made me sad to hear it.

During my interviews with Lisa, it took a while to peel away her many layers. For obvious reasons, it was hard for her to talk about being gay, having been raised in a traditional, religious family. It was even tougher revisiting her years battling food obsession and eating disorders. And sadly, retelling her horrible memories from Golf Channel took its toll on both of us. Though I never dealt with her specific issues, I've spent my entire life (including presently) battling those who would rather try to shut me up than hear me out and work to resolve conflict situations.

Out of all of Lisa's trials and tribulations, the one that I identify with most is her eating disorder. Entering high school at 14, I was significantly overweight. When I was measured and weighed for my physical to play basketball, the doctor told me I was already six feet tall but weighed 210 pounds. Bullies regularly zeroed in on me, mocking and shaming me for being fat. Girls that I liked consistently rejected my romantic overtures. Even parents, teachers, and so-called friends seemed to constantly rub my face in the fact that I was defective.

The one thing that has always stuck with me from that period of my life is how much my heart goes out to people struggling with obesity. Though women and minorities absolutely get the short end of almost every stick, in my opinion, fatphobia never gets enough scrutiny. No matter what physical issues people are dealing with, self-inflicted or medical, no one deserves to feel subhuman because of their physique. If anything, these folks need to be loved and encouraged to do what's best for their bodies and minds. We, the general public, need to call out fat-shaming just as loudly as racism, sexism, homophobia, ageism, classism—you name it.

Once Lisa and I connected all our dots, the trust and admiration for one another deepened. After Ben Strauss' article in the *Washington*

Post came out, I had him, Lisa, and Chelsea Kite on my podcast, which received some of the most fanfare of any episode I had released to that point.

What struck me most about Ben's interview was the exhaustive attention to detail he had to take for a respected publication like the *Washington Post* to run the story. He spoke about how important it was for him to be sure Lisa's allegations of institutional sexism were true. Ben spent months researching and verifying claims, making sure to have numerous sources confirm their credibility. He took these matters seriously, knowing that getting the information wrong would open him up to lawsuits and potentially ruin people's lives.

Ben Strauss went to those great lengths not just for a big story, but because he cared about the issues Lisa was addressing. He realized that what had gone on at Golf Channel before and during Lisa's time there was reprehensible and needed to be exposed. I admired his professionalism and willingness to take the slings and arrows that accompanied the article when it came out.

After the podcast, my writing partnership with Lisa bloomed into a dear friendship. I flew to Orlando and met her in person, and I got to follow Sarah Kemp around with Lisa during the 2021 U.S. Women's Open in San Francisco at the Olympic Club. Everything seemed to be on a straight upward trajectory. But my association with Lisa had caught the attention of some of the same key antagonist figures from the book. In the process of making lifelong friendships, I was simultaneously making powerful enemies, and it wasn't long before the Golf Channel ghouls came after me too. Within a day of our interviews being posted online, I received a direct message from Matt Ginella, now the CEO of an online media company called Fire Pit Collective:

> This is off the record. You know I appreciate and respect you.
> But this was a nothing story. Shocked the *Post* ran it. Happy
> to discuss further. Lisa had issues and none of them had to

do with being a female. What other examples in the story were relevant to current ownership/management? Everyone who crossed the line was dealt with. What am I missing?

I never agreed to keep our conversation off the record; regardless, he kept going. I quickly replied:

There is more I'm aware of that I can't discuss because I've been asked to keep it private. But suffice to say there's more bigger revelations forthcoming. Not my place to say but I know there are things in the works for Lisa and others that have reached out since the *No Laying Up* podcast. I'm always willing to hear you out Matt. Honestly just jumped on the interviews because it was an eye-popping story and I'm friends with Lisa.

"All good. Let's talk this week," Matt replied. I told him I was open to it and that we'd talk soon. Then silence. He never circled back about it. I had intentionally outed myself as Lisa's friend, and it was clear that he no longer trusted that I would believe his flimsy denial of the *Post* piece and allegations against her.

For a few months after that, we still acted distantly cordial to one another, but I knew it was only a matter of time before the bridge between us would be torched. That day was September 20, 2021.

That was the day Lisa and Matt got into their final Twitter battle, in which Ginella, Alan Shipnuck (another Fire Pit partner), and their cronies came looking for a fight. Without revisiting that chapter of the book too much, I watched as Lisa got tag-teamed by at least 30 men calling her everything from crazy and bitter to outright slandering her.

Some of the nastier comments from Ginella's cohorts:

Fire Pit Collective staff writer Laz Versailles tweeted, "It's fairly early to be drunk on a Tuesday. Not sure there's any other excuse for

@LisaMCornwell's actions here. Wrong on a few levels. This is sad, but I'm watching like it's my 600 lb. life."

Another user replied, "Careful talking about My 600 lb. life, she's going to think you're fat shaming her!"

Laz tweeted back, "I don't mess with alcoholics like that. I meant to say these fights (with men of clout) seems to be a constant in her life."

Alan Shipnuck joined in on the mansplaining: "Not everything is sexism, Lisa. That you're making a sad spectacle of yourself would be just as true if you were a dude."

Then an anonymous burner account shot out, "He calls you a crazy, bitter alcoholic because you are a crazy, bitter alcoholic."

Matt Ginella liked every one of those tweets, replying to them with more mockery and abuse, gassing them up more with every escalating tweet.

By this point in my relationship with Lisa, I had started feeling her pain when people called her awful names. Finally, after a tweet in which Matt called Lisa a "broken soul," I couldn't stay out of it anymore: "This is surely trolling Matt, no matter how you slice it... Do better."

I also replied to a few other people rebutting misinformation they had posted about Lisa's motives for speaking out against Golf Channel. Again, Ginella was right back in my DMs.

> **Matt:** You don't know all the facts. You have one side of a story that had two sides. I've explained this to you before. I'm sorry you're not seeing it or hearing it.
>
> **Me:** That's the thing—I'm trying to get to the bottom of the whole story—not just Lisa's side. In order to do so I need proof that she was indeed unprofessional and shitty at her work. Her performance reviews were flawless for seven years—most of the GC folks I've talked to love her and take

up for her character/professionalism. Honestly, you've been the main high-profile person publicly criticizing her. I can admit that I don't have the whole story—but as a journalist I want to know all the info—please help me make sense of the other side.

Matt: You're sincerely interested as in, this reporting for the book you guys are doing together?

The cat was out of the bag.

Me: Yes, I am helping her write her memoir. Yes, I'm sincerely interested in all the facts.

Matt: Reporting other reporter's info isn't being good at her job.

Me: When did that happen?

Matt: If you don't know that story, you aren't digging very deep. She came at me during Bethpage PGA, when I took exception to Daly driving a cart. I was in a heated Twitter battle over it and she came over the top defending him as a person, missing my point, which was related to his actions on the course. I went DM with messages to her, she wouldn't listen, I blocked her, and then she aired the fact that I blocked her publicly, making it look like it was only relating to our public tweets. I endured a massive amount of backlash over it. I went to GC over it. She eventually wrote me an email, apologizing, but the damage had been done. I've had countless people from GC and beyond thanking me for saying what they all wish they could say, which is, she's toxic, she's dangerous and she can't accept her role in why she's not there anymore. Making this a sexist issue is a convenient veil, but it's not true.

Me: Why did you block her for not listening? Did she insult you, call you names or something?

Matt: Because that's the way this works. You choose who can come to your party. At that time, given our DM's and the fact that she was ignoring my perspective and my points, it seemed like the right thing to do. That was between us. She went public with it. Trust me, no one caused a colleague more damage than what she caused me.

I knew it was my last chance to back down and kiss his feet. But I couldn't stop.

Me: But you were colleagues—seems like blocking was a rash move—also you said she apologized—and aren't you still employed by GC? Doesn't seem like it damaged your rep that much Matt. Were there other toxic moments? You claim lots of people feel that way. Who else had these types of run-ins with her (beside Brandel of course). Also: in what ways was Lisa dangerous at GC?

After that last round of questions: crickets.

We did not communicate for another 30 days. Our last DM exchange was on October 10, 2021. When I logged on to Twitter that day, I saw a post in which Ginella's handle had been tagged. Wondering what he had been up to since our last exchange, I clicked on the handle and looked at his page. He had unfollowed me.

I had hit a nerve.

Going for broke, I initiated the last round of DMs.

Me: I see you've unfollowed me. Such an odd way to play all of this Matt. I have given you shine on the podcast. Spoke up for Lisa after watching you and your guys shell her on

Twitter for almost a month (and yes you started it with the retweet chiding her for criticizing Molly—didn't say anything then—waited almost a month before simply asking you not to troll her. Never called you names. Asked reasonable questions when you DMed me and you left me hanging. Don't think detaching this way is a very good look, but so be it. Wish you well regardless.

Matt: I unfollowed because I didn't want to see any more sweaty workout pics. Not my thing. I had to laugh at the fact that you gave us "shine" on your podcast. I believe it was us who gave of our time. You're welcome. I've made several attempts to assist you in your reporting for these Lisa Cornwell memoirs. Good luck with that. We trolled Lisa? Another interesting take. You do you, Tucker. Good luck with that as well.

We've never spoken since.

Another somewhat ominous message popped up in my box shortly after the Ginella tête-à-tête. It was from a burner account with the handle @Robopz.

> **@Robopz:** You sure you want to publicly get involved in this? Just sayin.'
> **Me:** 50 women [came forward] Bud. That's a fact. Reported in the WaPo piece. Direct result of her interview with NLU. Women came out of the woodwork. I'm a big boy. I'll be fine.

> **@Robopz:** All I'll say…Bridges are tough to walk back across once they've been burned down…There's 2 sides to every story…Carry on…

I tried to ask who they were, but they would not give their name. Then, just as quickly as they'd jumped in my DMs, they were gone.

New unintended enemies aside, writing *Troublemaker* with Lisa has been a blast this year. Working with Lisa's feedback, I have grown immensely as a writer. She has introduced me to so many amazing people (most notably Sarah) and invested her money and time in me. But, even more so, her stories and insights have inspired me to take more accountability for my own subconscious sexist tendencies.

I am working hard to stop mansplaining. I also want to stop judging and sexualizing every woman I see, no matter how much advertisers and the mass media want to mesmerize me into doing. I will listen to women more, talk less, and try to believe them, even if their feedback is critical and uncomfortable. No matter how badly I want to be defensive, I know I'm often wrong, and critical feedback is tantamount to my survival in this world.

By no means do I think I am a chauvinist. I support the Time's Up and Me Too movements and think it's great that women are feeling more comfortable and compelled to speak out about their experiences. These brave ladies are doing the one thing that promotes actual change: applying public pressure on men to stop taking advantage of them.

Now I wish the world would speak louder about non-sexual issues—the microaggressions, the bullying, the powerful assholes, and their buddies who get away with crimes they pin on their victims. But more importantly, I want men to speak up for women too. While men may still rule most of the world, if these leaders would stick their necks out for women's and minority rights, holding violators accountable legally for their actions, things would change quickly.

Men like Geoff Russell, Matt Ginella, and Brandel Chamblee want women to look pretty, shut the hell up, and do what they're told. Any time women—or anyone who does not identify as male—defy this gender role, they are branded crazy, bitter bitches and forced to question their own sanity. It is textbook gaslighting. I have been guilty of this many times in my younger years and regret it every day.

From one fellow troublemaker to all you other troublemakers out there: dig in. Talk hard. There's much more work to be done.

ACKNOWLEDGMENTS

THERE ARE SO MANY PEOPLE I want to thank, but I have to start with the woman who not only lent her thoughtful words to this book but has been an inspiration for millions of women around the world, including me.

Hillary: Thank you for sharing your peanut butter with me that day in Little Rock. Thank you for always welcoming me with open arms. Thank you from the bottom of my heart for writing the foreword to this book. But, most of all, thank you for never being anything but yourself when those who couldn't break you privately tried to tear you down publicly. It has been a lesson in perseverance for us all. While your strength and smarts have been on full display for more than four decades, I've been fortunate to see your heart and humor behind the scenes my entire life. History will remember you for many great moments—most notably your speech in Beijing in 1995, when you boldly declared "...human rights are women's rights, and women's rights are human rights, once and for all." But, to me, your shining moment will always be those famous words from your concession speech in 2016: "To all the little girls watching..." Many years ago, I, too, was one of those little girls watching you closely—more than you probably realize—and I'm still watching in admiration and amazement to this day. Yes, it would've been an honor to call you Madam President. But it's an even greater honor to have your love, support, and friendship. That means more than I could ever express.

Tucker: You've become a pseudo-brother to me in this journey. From the first time we spoke, I knew you were the person I wanted *and needed* to help with one of my life's most challenging projects. As I've come to learn, writing a book isn't easy, but you're a gifted storyteller, and your talent was my guiding light throughout this process. For the last 20 months or so, you've made this book a priority. You've listened to my entire life story multiple times, shared your own story with me, and have gone to war with some of my social media antagonists—many of whom are mentioned in this book. I'll forever be grateful for your love and friendship and your willingness to trust me that this would happen. We made it!

Sarah: I'm not sure I could do anything without you and your love and support. While the last two years have thrown plenty of challenges our way, they've also brought us closer together. Thank you for giving me the time and space to work on this all hours of every day—or as you liked to call it, "Watching movies." Aussie, Max, Jazzy (forever), and I love you more than words can say. You've made my life complete.

Mom and Dad: I get emotional writing about you both. You're my heroes. I'm sure it wasn't easy to read about some of the things I kept from you for so long, but those experiences made me who I am today, and I don't regret any of them for one minute. My life's been amazing. Most importantly, you taught Tracy and me to be respectful, to treat people right, and to always stand up for ourselves and others. It's the greatest gift any parent can give to their child. I love you both so much and am beyond thankful that God blessed me with you as parents.

Tracy: You're my warrior. From the black leather miniskirt days to now, no one's ever had my back like my big sister. You have the biggest heart and fighting spirit of anyone I know. And, just like Mom and Dad, God has blessed me with you. Thanks for being there *anytime* I've ever needed you, without fail. I wouldn't have made it on my own. I love you so much, Trac, and I couldn't be prouder of you and the person you are…Bo and Olivia, too.

Allison: Where do I even begin? You've been a sister, best friend, psychologist, legal counselor, and voice of reason for most of my adult life. I don't know where I'd be if I didn't have you all these years, but it damn sure wouldn't have been the ride it's been without you. You're one of the true highlights of my life. Thank you for being exactly what I need every single time. I love you, AC.

Bill: If it hadn't been for you, this book would've been filled with a slew of four-letter words and regrettable anecdotes. You encouraged me early on to tell the story honestly, without pointing fingers as best I could, and let the reader decide where they landed with it. That advice led me to the path where I am today—less angry and less willing to engage with my detractors. Every time I talk to you, it's a life lesson. Thank you for your love and friendship all these years and for always being there when I need you. What a gift it's been.

Tom: You're the other brother I never had. Saying thank-you to you will never seem like enough. You not only believed in my case from day one but, more importantly, you believed in me. You were the perfect person I needed to handle this ordeal—intellectually, compassionately, and kickassingly. I'll forever be grateful to you for everything you've done and continue to do.

My five *amazing* aunts: Darlene, Katie, Marie, Nancy, and Martha. Just like my mom, throughout my life you've shown me what it truly means to be a strong woman. Your poor husbands never stood a chance. Thank you for your unconditional love and unwavering support. I love you all more than you know. You, too, Aunt Carolyn!

Jenny, Greg, Leisa, Jane, and Sarah's entire family in Australia: I hit the jackpot with my extended family "Down Under." I love you all and am very grateful for such a wonderful addition to my life!

Ed and Zac: You've been great friends for a long time—from my Faded Rose days to our many rounds of golf together. I'm not sure I'd love the game the way I do again if it hadn't been for you two. Thanks for your love and support. Laurie and Sarah, too! And to Henry and Frankie...I'm honored to be your godparent.

Teri Haskins: You steered the ship that literally turned my life around when I was completely lost at sea. I know I paid you to do it. But I also know how much you cared about me and my recovery throughout the process. I'll forever be deeply grateful for those years I spent with you in therapy. As hard as it was, I can honestly say that I wouldn't be where I am today without them... or you. You're my guardian angel, Teri. Thank you for your love and guidance.

Chelsea: We didn't know each other very well before all of this came out, but since then you've become a special person in my life. I'll forever be amazed by your strength and ability to smile through the pain. I hope that getting to share some of your story has helped ease it, even if just a little. You deserve that so much.

Anders and Nick: You reached out not long after I made my story public when no one else seemed interested in representing me. Having two respectable, honorable people tell me they believed in me and wanted to help meant the world, especially while I was mired in chaos. You've never waived in your belief in me for a moment during all of this, and that's something I'll never forget. Thank you both for your trust and friendship.

My "CME writer friend": I wouldn't have made it through this daunting writing process without your guidance. Thank you for always taking my calls and sharing your invaluable wisdom unequivocally.

Duff Daddy: You simply are the best. Much love to you, Jenny, Barbie, and the boys. Your love, friendship, and support mean more than Sarah and I could ever tell you.

Karen Crouse: From one woman in the sports media business to another, you get it. Thank you for being a friend and mentor in this process and for lending your sage advice along the way. You're a brilliant writer. I miss your voice in the golf world.

Netty: You're one heck of a trusted friend/advisor. Thank you for your friendship and taking the time to pore over this book before the actual editing process began. Awkwafina has nothing on you.

Chris Bodine: You've been a better friend than I've deserved. Thank you for your love, guidance, and support all of these years. Your heart is as big as your personality, and I'm grateful to have you as a friend.

Josh: Sarah and I think you're one of the best human beings on the planet! We love you and Shannon and appreciate your support in this journey more than you know.

Jerry Jones: Thank you for your sage advice throughout this project and so much more. You and Judy are good friends.

All of my coaches and teachers, especially Coach Kretschmar, Martha McNair, Dan Snider, Carol Clark, Jerry Hart, Dave Malone, and Steve Arnold: You taught me on the court, in the classroom, and on the course. But, mostly, you taught me in life. Thank you all for your influence and friendship. It's been a blessing to have learned from the very best.

All my friends at Fayetteville Country Club (past and present): Thank you for your support and friendship over the years. FCC will always be home and my favorite course in the world. Mary, Clyde, Boyd, Ron, and Vicki...we go back a long way and I love you all. I love you, too, Bill Agler. And, of course, Jerry, SuSu, and Steve forever.

The PGA Tour Live team: After speaking out, I never thought I'd work in golf media again. To be honest, I didn't know if I wanted to. You all not only embraced me as a person and a colleague, but you proved that the "no asshole policy" creates a great work environment. Even though I've never discussed this with anyone on the management team, it's obvious that egos and bad attitudes are left at the door. Thanks for the opportunities you've provided me and for making coming to work every day exactly what it should be—a privilege.

Triumph Books and my fantastic (and very patient) editor, Michelle Bruton: Thank you all for taking a chance on this book and on me. I'll forever be grateful. And to you specifically, Michelle— thank you for always taking my calls, answering every last question, making the book read much better, and teaching me what a "dinkus" is…ha! I've enjoyed every one of our conversations and appreciate you so much.

To all my family and friends: I love you and am grateful for you every day, even if we don't talk as much as we used to. Thank you for lifting me up more often than you realize.

And finally, to my fellow "troublemakers"—all the women who spoke up in the *Washington Post* article, including those who lent their names along with Chelsea: Jen Johnson, Haley Zagoria, and Laura Laytham; the women in the union who stood with us in solidarity; the men and women who reached out with their own stories of mistreatment; and those who reached out simply to show their support. You have no idea how much strength you gave me, especially during the most challenging time of my life. From the bottom of my heart, thank you all.

ABOUT THE AUTHORS

Lisa Cornwell spent seven years as an on-air host and reporter for Golf Channel, establishing herself as a respected voice in the game. Prior to Golf Channel, she worked in similar roles for the Big Ten Network as well as local affiliates in Mississippi, Tennessee, and Ohio. Lisa is a four-time Arkansas Women's State Golf champion, a two-time AJGA first-team All-American, a two-time All-State basketball player, and in 1992 was named the Arkansas Female Athlete of the Year. She was recently inducted into the Arkansas Golf and Arkansas Sports Halls of Fame.

Tucker Booth is a professional entertainer with a wide range of talents. Over the course of his career Tucker has been a writer, actor, comedian, singer, guitarist, pianist, DJ, and rapper. He has won 12 freestyle rap battle championships and is considered by many in his former hometown of St. Louis to be one of the city's best to ever do it. Tucker's podcast *Rappers Don't Golf* recently reached its 100th episode and has featured a variety of sports, music, and multimedia personalities. During the pandemic shutdown in 2020, Tucker wrote and recently published his first book, *Quick Trip*, which spans 25 years of wild misadventures he has had. Tucker now resides in Redondo Beach, California, with his wife, Charlotte, and son, Max. When he's not working on his creative endeavors, he spends his time volunteering at church and obsessing over Max's Little League pursuits.